The Power of ABCs

The Power of

Terry K. Shaw

Be blessed and enjoy your read!

A Guide to Unlock Your Inner Ceiba:

The Maya Cosmic Tree

The stories in this book are told from the author's perspective and reflect a personal recollection of experiences. Please note that there are sensitive contents and language that may trigger emotional reactions. The author used best judgment and knowledge to convey the information and insights as best as she could. All stories are not intended to distribute or share personal information about anyone. The practical tools contained in this book do not substitute for medical, financial, or legal advice. Use discretion and seek the assistance of such professionals. Identities and certain locations were modified to protect and respect privacy of individuals.

Book Design by Ryan Scheife, Mayfly Design
Cover Illustration by Brianna Gooch

To all souls looking for guidance on this mysterious, adventurous, and dynamic journey called life.

CONTENTS

AUTHOR'S PREFACE

Do you feel as if life is out of sync or out of control at times? That it is a tidal wave of struggles? A myriad of unavoidable interactions with others? A grid of uncertain tomorrows and lingering memories from past experiences? It is understandable if you answered yes. Our own reality, with its plot twists and turns, can spin us in a spiral of emotions filled with heartache, sadness, disappointments, pain, and regrets.

However, wait a second. Before you agree with any of that, let us try switching our whole thought process for a change. Before you accept that version of life as your truth, I ask you to examine your views and dig inwardly a little deeper. Ask yourself: *Is that how my life supposed to be? Or is that what my experiences have led me to believe? Can I change anything about how I'm living?* You certainly can change your reality by making a conscious effort to transform your own perspective and how you choose to create your life. In truth, isn't that why we are all here? To learn, create, grow, and expand?

We all must experience the world through people, places, and things. There is no way out of that. At times when my own life crumbled to pieces, as it has repeatedly along the way, I've asked God, the Creator, Source, the Universe—however you choose to describe it—to explain why everything feels so convoluted, so chaotic. The answers to my own unsolved puzzle arrived only when I stopped searching outside of myself. I had to turn inward and view the world through an inner lens, from my own soul's vantage point.

Our soul, or higher self, knows all the answers. It's our true nature: the part of ourselves that we became disconnected from to a greater or lesser degree. However, we can reconnect to who we are and change how we live our lives if we go within. But first we must become conscious of our own thoughts, words, and actions. If we remain unaware of our own creations, we will by default continue to experience life through our unconscious patterns.

The collection of thoughts and words fueling our internalized vocabulary, has either created better experiences or kept us stuck in cyclic loops, going nowhere. Fueled by emotions often correlated with pains or regret, our minds recreate more unwanted situations and patterns of behavior.

Now, the logical part of you may interject and say, "I've heard this all before. What's new?" Or, "Easier said than done." While it may seem that way, the real question you should ask yourself is: *have I truly applied my words consciously and wisely in my life—as ancient and modern sages already expressed?* As the Buddha said, "What we think, we become."

To illustrate the concept of the ABCs, this book goes in depth into the soul of the stories, words, and actions that often affect our experiences. This guidance tool has helped me to see the bigger picture beyond my own life's events, and I've personally incorporated the tools to assist in my own self-transformation. I ask that you open your mind and heart to the ideas shared in this book. Allow me to transmit some simple yet powerful wisdom while I guide you on a practical, magical, and spiritual journey through the heart and soul of Mother Nature.

Terry K. Shaw

A gentle tongue is a tree of life, but perverseness in it breaks the spirit.

Proverbs 15:4

THE BEGINNING

The Ceiba pentandra (pronounced SAY-buh), also known as the kapok or silk cotton tree, is a huge, majestic deciduous tree that grows in the subtropical and tropical rainforests in the Americas and west Africa and eastern Asia. The Ceiba can grow up to over 230 feet tall, with a varying lifespan of over 200 years old. It has elongated branches stretching above and beyond the canopy of the rainforest; a trunk armored with spiny thorns; and strong, buttressed roots seated deeply in and above Mother Gaia.

In modern Maya culture and ancient mythology, the Ceiba tree is a symbolic representation of the Maya cosmic tree of life (or Ya'axché, meaning "first green" in the Yucatec Mayan language), connecting all living and non-living aspects of the Maya universe. The Maya believed the horizontal branches were connected to the thirteen heavenly realms, the straight, spiny trunk was part of the earthly realm, and the strong roots were part of the nine-level underworld, Xibalba, where life sprouted.

You may have heard of such sacred, mystical trees in other world mythologies and belief systems, such as the acacia tree in ancient Egypt, the crann bethadh in Celtic traditions, or the Bodhi tree, where the Buddha attained enlightenment. Most or all conceptions of divine, spiritual trees carry meanings as symbols of life, rebirth, creation, growth, and balance. All share a deep connection to our lives.

Everyone has their own inner Ceiba, as I term it, which is a subtle representation of our internalized and externalized vocabularies, consisting of the thoughts and words driving our current beliefs and perceptions about life. Let's explore the deeper connection of your inner Ceiba to your experiences, words, and self-expansion.

Raise your words, not voice. It is rain that grows flowers, not thunder.

JALAL AL-DIN RUMI, PERSIAN POET

YOUR INNER CEIBA

Like the rainforest, which serves as the birthing ground for other trees, wildlife, and plants, our inner Ceiba is the home to our own life's experiences, which are influenced by our family, friends, and everyone else around us. They are the main contributing factors affecting our inner balance, peace, and happiness. Branch to branch, root to root, everyone works in an interconnected web of communication through thoughts, words, emotions, and habits, as part of the co-creative process. However, somewhere along our transitional phases of growths and lessons, we've fallen into traps of our own stories and negative thought and word patterns. Yet we can always transform those stories if we choose.

The Ceiba tree has strong buttressed roots, a long and spiny trunk, and powerful, horizontal branches with large leaves, fruits, and flowers. Our inner Ceiba follows a similar structure and consists of four simple elements: the branches of ABCs, rooted experiences, trunk insights, and leaves of healing.

The interconnected branches are your ABCs—the redefined words of wisdom used as a quick reference guide. The rooted experiences are the memories of past events streaming within the subconscious and conscious mind. The trunk insight is the pathway from the roots to the branches, which transforms those lingering experiences into powerful insights gained in order to grasp the lessons learned. Finally, the branches house leaves of healing, which offer practical, transformative tools to reprogram your thoughts and words back into alignment with your true self. This is where we aim to bloom flowers of new beginnings and bear fruits of better experiences.

A. The Branches of ABCs

The branches of ABCs are twenty-six meaningful, interconnected words, forming the umbrella-shaped crown of your inner Ceiba. They spread across the canopy of your life and serve as highway of emerging definitions, connecting to the source of light and empowerment. The more you align your vocabulary with these words of wisdom, the more easily you can navigate through your life's journey.

The branch definitions are shortened descriptions that serve as takeaways for quick reference. They provide redefined meanings for words in your vocabulary that have been mis-defined with negative connotations based on past experiences. For instance, *love* may often manifest as difficult and hurtful, but the common definition (in layman's terms) has limited it to a specific experience. The word *different* can often mean weird or oddball and may promote feelings of non-inclusion.

There are two forms of application for our ABCs: verbs (V) and adjectives (A):

(V): The action form of the word. The process of applying the definitions we created. No experience is worthwhile without applying the concepts fully. Words mean everything in action. As spiritual guru Osho once said, verbs are, "rather than being, think becoming."

(A): The descriptive feeling of becoming. The more descriptive we are with our words, the more our subconscious minds register them as truths. All adjectives use the sacred syllable "I AM" to emanate the powerful vibration connected to our true sovereign self. When you utter "I am love" on a regular basis, you are transmitting a powerful signal to yourself that you are a divine essence of God. We only *become* as we define ourselves with pure intent and trust.

B. Rooted Experiences

The Maya believed that the Ceiba sprang to life from the under-world, which is located at the roots. At the roots of our inner Ceiba are the rooted experiences that shaped how we live today. Yet some of our rooted experiences became the main influencers of our vo-cabulary, which tends to carry limited and conditioned definitions of words we often hold as truth. They are the ones we repeat, or have given much of our energy to, and they help shape the vaguely defined, emotionally fueled words of fear connected to our past experiences.

The problem is that our inner dialogue is still lingering here— barely moving beyond the trunk. This limits us from living our true potential and achieving real freedom within ourselves. We have given much power to the temporary nature of past negative ordeals and circumstances, keeping us mentally blocked, full of worries and distrust. The purpose of the root is to give you strength and stability to expand, to get past feeling trapped and afraid to move forward with your life.

The root is as important as the branches in our inner Ceiba, for without roots there are no branches, hence no progression or growth. We cannot discount the fact that past experiences have in-fluenced our present reality, but they are not the true essence of who we are as souls. Our experiences should only serve as a foun-dation of persistence, to help us raise our level of consciousness. We can create a better story by embracing the roots as insights and lessons as we flow upwards on the trunk.

C. Trunk Insight

In its youthful stage, the trunk of the Ceiba tree has sharp, conical thorns to protect it and ward off animals from feeding on its bark. However, over the years, as it grows and expands in its environ-ment, the thorns smooth out and disappear.

As we learn and grow from life's lesson, our journey can flow smoothly beyond the thorns of obstacles and struggles if we approach them from an open and different perspective. The alchemical nature of our inner Ceiba's trunk is to provide useful insights to serve as an integral pathway between the experiences at the roots and heightened awareness at the branches.

Only we can understand and define what serves us or what we must let go of to improve our lives. How do you react to a past memory that resurfaces? Do you focus on the negative aspects of the situation? Or do you reaffirm yourself as a powerful creator who has changed for the better? To move beyond the rooted experiences, you must treat them as blessings of lessons that will help you transcend to the branches, where healing can happen.

D. Leaves of Healing

On the branches of our ABCs are the leaves of healing, which *serve as a source of self-transformation*. The book of Revelation, 22:2, speaks of the tree of life, where the "leaves of the tree were for the healing of the nations." Through the utterance of our ABCs lies a powerful source of transformation in order to rebalance our mind, body, and soul back into love and wisdom.

The purpose of the leaves is to nourish our minds with intentions and transform lingering experiences into an abundance of peace, joy, or whatever you decide for yourself. Your words can heal and release negative emotions if you open your mind and heart to your own inner power. The leaves can be embraced as affirmations, prayers, mantras, chants, decrees, invocations, or any other modality. They are all important tools to fuel divine transformation from within.

The concept of the power of ABCs is straightforward. Do you realize how powerful you are, even with the simple expression of the words you utter from your mouth? The message here is simple: it is time to take back control of your life using the inspiring nature of your words.

Are you ready? Are you truly ready to apply yourself to create a better journey that gives you authority over your own life's experiences? Follow along with me as I share my own personal and transformative journey, which may assist you in unlocking your own inner Ceiba.

IS FOR ACCEPT

Branch Ac·cept (V): Acknowledge and face your own experiences. Transform your mindset from fear into unconditional love for yourself. Return to your true natural essence of self.

Rooted Experience: *What experiences have you not accepted?*

The Brooklyn night flickered with dimming stars in the distant sky, while a looming darkness engulfed my thoughts. Anger, confusion, and shame pierced my heart like the protruding thorns on the trunk of a young Ceiba.

Why me, God? I sobbed with both hands clenched tight as rage rushed through my veins. *What have I done to deserve this?* I released my grip to wipe the tears flowing down my weary face. In silence and despair, I sat in a cold, detached garage behind my shared apartment complex while I replayed the events that had unraveled three hours earlier.

"Didn't I tell you to call me before and after you leave school?" His voice echoed in a calm sternness.

"I did call you, but I had to catch the train. You know how rush hour is." My nerves began to fray as I knew he would make a drama out of this.

"You don't listen to me, and now you have to suffer for this." As my boyfriend's words seeped through my mind, I gasped in anger as he showed me the door.

"Sleep outside until you learn your lesson." His words flooded fear through my blood. *Hell no! Not again! I'm not doing this anymore!* I scrambled in my mind for my next moves to avoid being kicked outside yet again.

Fighting my way back into our living space, I tried to prevent him from taking control of me, but he was too strong and blocked every attempt I made. With a bruised arm and heart, I gave in—as always.

Disgruntled I sat in the shadows of the garage tools, asking God for a sign that I should move out. In total embarrassment, I hid myself in the darkness, hoping not to alert the landlord or the neighbors, who were in and out of the complex. Fear shook my hands. Desperation set in as I cried for answers from God. At the same time, a vengeful and hurtful part of myself concocted a revenge plot to make his life a living inferno.

I visualized myself kicking the door in and giving him a dose of his own medicine. I also visualized a quiet conversation where he and I would discuss our relationship issues and he would listen to how I felt for a change. *Who am I kidding?* I snapped myself back to the disastrous reality I was living in, as a wave of disempowerment and weakness flooded in.

No more of this! I sat upright with my shoulders high after regaining the little strength I had after all the bawling I'd done. But my mind kept reliving the good times we had shared. The strong sexual attraction. The financial support I received. The hopes that one day he would say, "Will you marry me?" On the other end, my heart and soul screamed for mercy and freedom—far away from his emotional and mental entrapment. All hopes seemed lost, as there was no way to change the fact that I was already in this domestic hell.

You must move on, an inner voice whispered, but moving on was beyond my comfort zone. I was already on bad terms with my family—there was no one to call and no friends to confide in. All efforts seemed pointless at that stage. Nonetheless, I knew I had to make the move somehow, someway, before any further drama manifested into the worst.

A few months after this tumultuous disagreement, I left him and took my baggage packed with anger, regrets, and bitterness. I had no plans to turn back.

But nine years later I was in another compromising predicament. The cops stood by the doors of my new apartment as they took statements about the altercation between me and a new lover.

"What did you think? The cops were going to save you?" He smirked after they departed the scene. I smiled with an aching tiredness inside, but the gloomy daytime sky beamed with intense clarity. I was drained and emotionally detached. This time around, there were the added bonuses that I was not asking God "Why?" or sitting in anyone's garage. The decision to move on was clearer than ever.

Something is off here, I thought after another wearisome move. Yes, I was more confident. Yes, I was stronger. Yes, I was bolder. But some wisdom was still missing in this unrequited love equation. My eyes opened to the understanding that the last drama mirrored the first drama I thought I'd rid myself of. Perplexed and confused, I turned to the only person who could give some account of what was happening in my love life: *Why do you keep attracting the same type of relationship, Terry?*

After years of self-reflection as a single woman, I discovered my own misconstrued perceptions about men and myself. My beautiful, precarious mind played fantasy-like stories about how a relationship should work: *If I had given him more attention, maybe he would love me better. I am lonely and incapable of finding true love. I just want to make him happy and be nice.*

Unbelievable! I listened to the negative thought patterns on a broken record of memories. A bit embarrassed, I listened to myself also replay childhood events when a family member had predicted, "When you grow up your man is going to beat you." I'd never realized or believed that even such a comment would later play out as an experience—but it did. The harsh self-awareness of my own negative thoughts was a hard pill to digest.

Deep down, I wanted change. Deep in my soul, I wanted peace. Deep in my heart, I wanted to be loved by someone who understood, loved, and accepted me. Yet as I asked God for these things, I also realized that I had not changed. I had no peace, nor did I understand, love, or accept my own self.

Reality struck hard with these inconvenient truths.

However, I did not give up on love. That would mean giving up on myself. Coming face to face with the reality I had unconsciously created was frightening but helped me to release the mental and emotional baggage I carried from my past relationships. Letting go of the past meant accepting the dark aspects of my own faults and my pride by acknowledging the role I had played in my attempts at finding love. As I let go of my old stories, I attained a pearl of undeniable wisdom from my own shortcomings with no self-judgment nor regrets. I knew I was more than what I had experienced, and I was determined to end these toxic cycles masquerading as love. And as I accepted myself, other branches of forgiveness, trust, and—most importantly—honesty, extended into my life. I learned to walk the path back to the true essence of who I am.

Trunk Insight: *Accept That You Are More Than Your Experiences*

Accepting ourselves is the alpha of our journey back to our true essence of self—our divine source of love, truth, wisdom, and strength from within. Yet accepting is also one of the most difficult branches to walk. What we cannot accept repeats itself in some form or another until we face it with openness and understanding to make the necessary changes for our personal growth.

Many of us have not expanded to the other branches of our inner

Ceiba because we have given so much focus to certain negative experiences in our lives. At times, we seek some form of validation from another person, hoping they can provide us the affection we desire. Yet, in truth, the acceptance we seek already dwells within us.

It is not our fault, nor is it the fault of anyone else, that we repeat the same patterns of behavior. Nonetheless, we must acknowledge and change what is not working well in order to create better things for ourselves. If we allow our minds to keep us trapped at the roots of negative inner dialogue, then we are blocking the powerful transformations waiting to bloom new beginnings into our lives. Accept who you are beyond what life has shown you. Allow the guiding light within to illuminate the path toward heightened awareness in yourself. You are meant to become so much more than what you held onto. Let go and allow the profound changes to permeate your being.

Life is about transformation and becoming. Change is inevitable and necessary for progression. Each experience, whether good or bad, serves as a transition period onto a newer path of becoming more powerful in yourself. With an open mind and heart, consider your setbacks or mistakes as your growth toolkit for life. Because as one experience ends, another one is in the process of rumination, and whatever event transpires in your reality depends on your perception and belief systems. Are you aware that you can direct the script to a better story?

It is important to be aware of the paths you are consciously creating with your thoughts, words, and actions. Saying *I will never be happy* or *If I had known better* will not change the outcome of an event that led to a negative manifestation. The storms have passed. Address them, and set them free by making a change for the better in your life. Real change within takes immense confidence and courage but also involves letting go of our own ego's will to control everything. Accept responsibility for your actions and start creating better for your own peace and happiness.

Make peace with your past and every passing experience along your way. You can either use the lessons to attain inner freedom and strength or hold onto the pain and suffering and stay stagnant on the same hamster wheel. Reap your lessons as blessings, not as regrets or blame. The insights gained from your experiences are necessary to broaden your horizon so that you never settle for anything less than you deserve.

Embrace the changes from within and allow God to guide you back to your true essence of self. You never know what wisdom you may discover when you reconnect with the essential core of who you are. Your true self does not merely exist. It lives and flows naturally with every situation that shows up. Your true self embraces every present moment by grasping even the worst experiences as wisdom. Your true self accepts all versions of you and others as is. It holds no judgment, no fears, no limiting beliefs about your past ordeals. It understands the bigger picture beyond your experiences. You can attain immense clarity, all-encompassing wisdom, and fruitful knowledge when you accept and embrace your true divine self.

You are not your past. What happened to you is not an indication of who you truly are. Release the excuses or fears and move on with anticipation that the best is yet to come. Rise above the negative connotations and definitions you may have unconsciously fed your mind. The courage and strength that propel you to move inwards are the same God-given qualities necessary in elevating your thoughts and words to another level of expansion. Accept who you are, let go of the old stories you have held onto, and allow your overdue metamorphosis to unfold naturally. Your soul has been waiting for this moment. Are you ready to receive your divine transformation?

Leaves of Healing: *Acceptance of Self Affirmations*

Like the Ceiba branches stretching over the canopy of the

rainforest, accepting yourself opens the path to personal transformation. When you accept yourself and others, you will be propelled to a heightened awareness of becoming more than your obstacles and trials. Be willing to release and let go of past experiences which no longer define or serve you. Connect with your true self by going within as you realign with the truth of who you are becoming.

Take a moment to breathe in deeply and then breathe out any heavy energy of fear, self-judgment, or regret. Rub both of your hands together to gather the powerful energy from your soul. Place your left hand over your heart and raise your right hand to engage in a pledge of allegiance. This time around, the pledge is to accept yourself. Read the below affirmation three times, and as you do this, envision yourself walking along the branch of Acceptance with courage and understanding. The path to a profound transformation within is illuminated when you open your heart to accept yourself.

I accept my experiences and let go of worries and fears.

I accept the truth of who I AM connected to my true self.

I accept the divine love guiding me towards change.

IS FOR BEAUTIFUL

Branch Beau·ti·ful (A): Calm-natured. A kind and composed demeanor. Remain graceful even when others try to bring your spirit down.

Rooted Experience: *Has someone ever made you feel less than beautiful?*

In my sophomore year in college, I worked as a sales associate for Victoria's Secret, known for its beautiful supermodels, sexy lingerie, and sweet perfumes. Like any other business, working in retail had its highs and lows, especially when dealing with a plethora of customers from all walks of life. While some were friendly, others were not so open and welcoming. Nonetheless, I did my best to provide the best customer service as I navigated the different personalities I encountered.

Then again, there are moments when someone tries to push you over the edge—at least if you allow them.

The rush of the summer sales season had customers flocking like geese into the store to take advantage of the huge bargains on panties and bras. It was a busy Saturday afternoon, and my usual assigned area in the front section of the store was given to other colleagues. That day, I was placed in a less hectic area at the back to assist in boosting sales of an unpopular name brand of lingerie. I was happy to dodge the bullet that was the chaos up front.

Geez, I spoke too soon. I smiled at the three ladies rushing towards me. They panted heavily in what seemed like a major beauty crisis.

"We need your help ASAP!" They gasped for air.

"I need a nude no-show panty for an evening gown for tonight. Let me show you the picture. Please tell me you have something. Please," one of the ladies expressed in frustration. Instantly, as I looked at the photo, I knew what she wanted and was ready to sell without hesitation.

"Please follow me, ma'am." I led her and her friends to the table of beautiful shades of nude, black, and white underwear.

"I think these are what you are looking for. These seamless nude panties work perfectly under your dress. What's your size?"

"Medium," She replied, and turned to her two friends, who nodded in agreement.

Searching under the table, with buckets loaded with different sizes and colors, I realized we had no nude panties left on the sales floor. With her mouth pouted, she shrugged her shoulders with impatience and annoyance.

"Ok, let me check our stockroom. Maybe they have a few left. Give me one moment." I radioed down to the stock associates but received a response that we were entirely out of stock in those colors. *Damn! Think fast Terry. She's getting agitated.*

A light bulb turned on.

"There are always other color options you can try." Improvising on my sales pitch, I grabbed a black panty off the top table and explained how it worked perfectly under any attire. The woman turned to her friends and laughed aloud. Confused at her laughter, I looked to her friends, who seemed confused as well.

"I am sorry, honey. Black does not work for me. It is not my skin tone."

A huge gulp disrupted the flow of my breathing. I swallowed hard and smiled passively at the ignorance in her comment. *Wait, am I blowing this out of proportion? Should I take this as an insult?* I thought to myself with a plastic grin plastered across my face. I brushed it off as nothing.

"Oh, please allow me to show you how it works." Confident in my sales skills, I placed the black panties under a nearby white silk robe to demonstrate how they were the Jane-of-all-trades.

In her own illustration, she took the underwear from my hands and placed them next to my skin. "No honey, it's not going to work. You are just as black as these panties. They will work for you, not me."

"Isn't she as black as these panties?" she turned to her friends. They looked away in what seemed to be utter disbelief.

My heart rate pounded at her racist remark, as a surge of anger triggered old memories about my own insecurities in my skin complexion. Memories of being told by my peers, in my earlier school years, that I was the blackest in the class. Memories of a family member offering me bleaching cream for my face. My mind raced like horses, bridled with curse words and a clenched fist. In that moment, I felt less than beautiful. But an inner voice uttered, *Choose your next words with grace.*

"Is there anything else I can assist you with?" My smile widened as a wave of adrenaline rushed through me. With a smirk, she shook her head with an abrupt *no.* Embarrassingly enough for her, one of her friends pulled me to the side and apologized for her rudeness. *I am not allowing this lady to ruin my day,* I said to myself as I took a deep breath and walked away to assist another customer.

Did I think about my job? No doubt—I needed to pay my bills. Did it bother me? Absolutely—I am human. Even though her racist remarks dampened my thoughts, they did not affect my soul. I was proud after releasing myself from the stench of her own ignorance.

While I didn't meet the sales goal of the day, I did meet a better side of myself. Overall, I felt a renewed energy of inner strength and calmness because I never reacted in anger as much as I wanted to. It was a victorious moment knowing that I never allowed her to bring me down to any level lower than what she may have intended. I chose to show her that true inner beauty was priceless and unde-fined by the color of any panty.

There is a legendary Maya story which tells the tale of two beautiful women who lived in a village on the Yucatan Penin-sula, Mexico. One woman—called Xkeban, translated to mean "bad woman"—who seduced men for sexual pleasures. The other woman—called Utz-colel—behaved virtuously and was a virgin.

The villagers viewed Xkeban as a lustful woman due to her al-luring actions with men. Yet she had a pure and kind heart and gave to all in need of assistance. She helped the poor, the homeless, and the stray animals within the village. On the other hand, Utz-colel was mean and arrogant and belittled the poor, the weak, and the homeless.

One day, Xkeban died, and no one knew until the scent of a sweet, perfume-like flower called, xtabentún, exuded from her home. The pleasant aroma, flowing from her heart, drew the atten-tion of the villagers, even Utz-colel. When Utz-colel smelled the fragrance, she judged Xkeban's scent as impossible, since Xkeban was "impure and unclean" from engaging in sexual encounters with many men. Utz-colel professed that her scent would be sweeter than Xkeban's when she departed the earth.

When Utz-colel died, everyone showed up to her funeral to pay respect for her virtuous way. However, a rancid stench like that from a spiny cactus flower, tzacum, fumed from her grave.

The smell from Utz-colel's heart was unbearable and repul-sive to the villagers. They noticed that Xkeban's kind and loving heart blossomed into beautifully scented flowers while Utz-colel's cold and mean heart emitted a pungent odor. Utz-colel embraced "beautiful" by appearance but not by nature. The power of Xkeban's beauty bloomed from her heart, with a loving grace of kindness, despite how the villagers viewed her.

The essence of true beauty lies within the heart of our very existence, which is defined not by our hair or skin tone or body type but rather by our soul's loving nature. True beauty never arises from judgment and intolerance of others. It simply outshines negativity with the light of grace and kindness. When you stand firm in your truth, the beauty of your soul will overpower negative remarks and judgments. Let your true beauty radiate in truth and patience.

What is physical beauty? It's nothing of substance when our minds are reeking with thoughts of hatred because of skin complexion and our hearts are drowning in mud of bitterness towards another person because we refuse to accept what they look like. Do not allow someone's words or actions to change who you are because they cannot accept the shade of your skin, the length of your hair, or your body size. There is no need to change any aspect of yourself to please anyone. The Divine made you perfect just the way you are. Never allow others to dim your shine with words of fear and discrimination. Be patient and set boundaries with those individuals whose minds are still sleeping in the shadow of themselves.

When your inner beauty speaks, it radiates confidence and surety amid ridicules, giving you the ability to react wisely. What you exert in any scenario is in your control and power. You control the outcome when you emotionally detach yourself from others' opinion about your physical appearance. In the heat of any situation, remember who you are. There are always other options to expunge negativity if you allow your soul to take charge.

Your soul eradicates any feelings of low self-esteem because of someone else's lack thereof. What others say and do is merely a reflection of their own fear of not accepting the visible differences in others. Pitch love to the ones who have mistreated, oppressed, or criticized you. They may be lacking these qualities in the roots of their own life's experience. Give them a different reaction from what they may be used to, with patience and kindness. It may be difficult at first but necessary for your own inner growth and expansion. Show them the full embodiment of true beauty by embracing the humble part of yourself.

When you allow yourself to blossom from the inside out, you emit a smell of perfume that sweetens any experience. Only you can unlock your inner beauty, so never allow anyone to dim your self-confidence or redefine who you are. You have the power to choose what you allow to capture your energy.

Any fear exerted by another person, based on their own perception of you, should only reaffirm your own uniqueness and empowerment. As you embrace your true self, you can only expand upwards on the branch of becoming more beautiful in God's love. Remember this: a true beauty thrives for inner progression, not external perfection. Choose your next word and reaction wisely in order to serve your highest good.

Leaves of Healing: *Blooming Beautifully Affirmations*

Close your eyes for a moment. Imagine yourself walking through a luscious, tropical rainforest where the sun radiates through the canopy of a tall, majestic Ceiba tree. Sit at the edge of the tree, where the bountiful bromeliads, orchids, and passion flowers dance in the breeze. Move your hands through them in a soft motion. Hold the flowers close to your heart and smell the sweet fresh fragrance they naturally release. Breathe in the nurturing energy of Mother Nature. She is the essence of your true beauty. As you inhale the scents, feel the flow of beauty surrounding you. Get in touch with the core of who you are and say the below kind words to yourself.

I am a beautiful soul on the path of becoming.

I am beautiful within.

I am a beautiful soul on the path of true knowing.

I am beautiful without.

Use this affirmation often as a reminder that you are a beautiful soul of divine light and love.

IS FOR CENTER

Branch Cen ⋅ ter (V): Maintain balance while you navigate the reality of life. Aim to create more harmony within your mind, body, and soul for your own personal well-being, happiness, and growth.

Rooted Experience: *Do you feel an imbalance in any area of your life?*

After I graduated from college in 2010, the uncertainty in finding a job in New York City lessened my hopes of securing a strong career. During that period, the unstable nature of the US economy continued to straggle on from the 2008 financial crisis. For many new college graduates like myself, job prospects seemed out of reach and hopeless. Yet "Superwoman," my I-can-do-it-all persona, was determined and ready to sacrifice whatever it took to become successful. It did not matter what was happening in the economic landscape.

Nine months after starting my job search, I landed my first full-time position as a finance assistant at a prominent college in New York City. As a young and driven twenty-two-year-old, starting out in such a position was a major deal, considering I had little work experience in the accounting field. Over the years, I worked hard and managed to shift into higher level roles. By the time I was twenty-eight, I was at the pinnacle of career success. Life was more than I had dreamed of.

Wow, I cannot believe how far I've come, I acknowledged, while fantasizing about my next steps in life during an office meeting related to the new budget plans for the department. I was grateful to God for what I had created for myself, yet a bit worried about the way I was building my life.

There were many factors at play as I tried to balance life around me. A newly formed marriage. Plans to start graduate school. A full-time job. A long list of to-dos with goals and plans, which seemed never-ending.

How long can you manage these piles of responsibilities? I asked myself, while scribbling circles on the reports I should have been reading. *Can you handle this marriage?* I realized that I barely even saw my husband every day. *There's no way you can start graduate school within the next two years.* I battled at the crossroads of my mind between economics and accounting degrees. The mental inquisition showed no mercy as I tried to analyze the layouts of the new financial processes.

Grrrrr. A loud roar from my stomach interrupted the silence in the room. My stomach churned with an unbearable discomfort, reminding me of another important factor I neglected in the process of creating my new life.

As I juggled career and personal obligations, I was medically diagnosed with H. pylori, a bacterial infection found in the digestive tract. The many nights of excruciating abdominal pains and a severe stomach ulcer drove me into insomnia and gave me anxiety attacks. The health issues affected my work and mental performance and made it difficult to eat the foods I loved. Ben and Jerry's ice cream. Jerk chicken. Oxtail. All became big no-nos on my list of favorite treats.

Living life the way I planned became more complicated than easier.

Even though my doctor treated me, I still feared the worst. I could not help but to think back on the host of Google searches on "What is H. pylori?"

I gulped in fear as I perused an online article—"Difficult to treat"—while, palms sweaty, I rolled the mouse to scroll through the search results. *Dear God, am I dying?* My eyes popped wide open while watching an online video on stomach infections. Fears escalated to misery when I recalled a conversation with my mother about our family lineage and the many digestive issues we faced.

"Chile, please. Your great-grandfather had some serious stomach issues. You must watch what you eat. I ain't playing, chile," she warned after experiencing her own shares of horrible digestive setbacks. Flashing back to my tween years in Jamaica, I also recalled a series of ulcer episodes corroding the lining of my grandmother's digestive tract. She belched uncontrollably in agony for several months. I remembered how my family members' health had unraveled, and it appeared to be the path I would travel, too, if I didn't change how I lived my life.

Deep down I knew I had to change that person who stared at me in the mirror every morning. But stubbornness was my kryptonite. As a result of my actions, chaos interjected to stir my life out of balance. I became stressed and overwhelmed from pushing my limits.

Not only was my work life in need of a complete overhaul, but my personal life stumbled close to the edge of oblivion. My marriage dwindled to dust as all communication between us blew off with the wind. My application to enroll in one of the top graduate accounting programs in New York was rejected instead of accepted as planned. *Damn, everything around me is falling apart. There's just too much going on!* Frankly, I failed to factor in my life's goals: *Take care of your inner well-being and happiness above everything else.* The imbalance wreaked havoc in my physical, emotional, mental, and spiritual existence.

Taking a step back, I prayed to God for inner guidance to reassess every goal, every course of action, and every possible path towards centeredness. Rebalancing my life meant canceling the variables that no longer served my personal growth and development.

Admittedly, it was difficult to leave my long-standing job of eight years, move states as a divorcée, and revamp my diet from red meat to mostly veggie dinners. However, it was all worth the reconnection to God and my true self. In letting go of those old ways of existing, I attained a deeper sense of inner joy and happiness in living. And when life's circumstances threw me off the balancing scales of reality, I reaffirmed to myself: "I am centered with God in my mind, body, and soul."

Trunk Insight: *Center Yourself Everywhere in God*

The ancient Maya considered the roots, trunk, and branches of the Ceiba tree as an interconnected system of balance and flow emulating the natural cycles of life. Each element serves different purposes, but they all work together to support the growth and expansion of the giant cosmic tree. If one element becomes imbalanced, then the whole system is affected.

The elongated branches cannot balance themselves horizontally without the support from the buttressed roots holding the tree firmly to the ground. The creatures cannot climb the branches without the bridging support of the trunk, which also transports water from the roots to the branches. To continually grow and expand, the Ceiba is centered not only in itself but with every tree, plant, and creature in its environment. And if the soil is unstable and lacks foundation, even the mighty Ceiba falters during storms, affecting everything in its surroundings.

As we already know, our physical lives are not built like trees. Movement is our driving force. Action is our way to attain what we desire. But as we engage in our daily activities, balance is needed within all facets of our being. It should permeate our mind, body, and soul. And if we continue to live on the edge of survival every day, chaos will intervene to cause a ruckus in different areas of our lives.

There are days when we may feel as if our lives are a race against time and to-do lists. If it is not our work, then it is school or home. If it is not our family, then it is our friends or other people. If it is not us, then it is everything else around us. Finding harmony can feel overwhelming when most days seem to be running by swiftly as we chase dreams and desires.

Not every day can we accomplish our bulleted, outlined plans and get what we want. Not every day will be a clear horizon with the sun shining brightly in our lives. However, if we understand our own power to recreate a more stable experience, we can realign the wheel of balance back to harmony in our mind, body, and spirit. If we do not acknowledge and address the imbalances existing in our lives, chaos will arise, reminding us to change and return to our natural state of living.

Chaos shows up everywhere; accept it. As much as we plan our lives, confusion will reveal itself through our creations or from unexpected turns of events. With its many faces, stress can drain us physically, emotionally, spiritually, and mentally. Nonetheless, these challenges can also empower and strengthen us to make changes if we dance and flow with them. Amid chaos, we must realize our inner power to transform our current situations and take the necessary action steps to rebalance ourselves and move forward. The more we let go of the controls, the easier it becomes to return to a centered state of being and to allow the transformations to take its natural course.

Change is inevitable; embrace it. What would this life be if we saw everything coming in plain sight? As the Greek philosopher Heraclitus stated, "Hidden harmony is better than obvious harmony." Change is inevitable and can feel frightening and unbearable, but if you allow your mind to stir fears about the unknown, then change will be difficult to face and endure. This process is necessary for us to evolve and expand onto the path to heightened awareness and inner harmony. Adjust to the changes with ease by embracing them with confidence and an inner knowing that all is well with God.

Center is everywhere; become it. Greek philosopher and poet Empedocles once stated, "The nature of God is a circle of which the center is everywhere and the circumference is nowhere." Circumstances will take you off track into unwanted experiences, and when that occurs, consult your higher self to move forward into a direction of inner knowing and trust. Connect with the light within in order to shift your thoughts to more conscious creations. Reevaluate and resolve the imbalances in the areas of your life that are not working well. To reach the real center of yourself, you must start within you, not at the equilibrium of external outcomes or pursuits. Anchor your life with God in your plans by realigning yourself in the present moment through gratitude.

Remember, you are the star in this matrix. Do you want to continue being the juggler of to-do lists in a wild circus, or the director of more flowing experiences? You control how much weight you place on your shoulders. You decide which way the scales will slide for your benefit, so take charge of the situations that are tipping you over the edge into stress and anxiety. You can only grow and expand when you aim to change the imbalances. Choose to create better for yourself to extend your vitality and longevity. Know that a life without balance is merely existing and not living in its true essence.

Leaves of Healing: *Center Your Life Affirmations*

Are you feeling tired, lost, confused, overwhelmed, or stressed? Take inventory of the areas of your life that are not working well. Your soul is calling you to change something. Stop and listen to what it is saying. Now, close your eyes and breathe in peace, harmony, and bliss. Exhale exhaustion, control, and stress. Do this activity three times to get the movement in your body flowing. Now ask yourself, "What do I need to do to rebalance this specific area of my life?" Be open and receptive to the answers. They will show up when you least expect it. As you recognize where the imbalances exist, make a list of what you can do to adjust it. Changes do not happen overnight. They require effort on your part. Be willing and ready to put in the work. To get you started with the process, affirm that "I am already centered" in those areas of your life that are out of sync and stagnant at this time.

I am centered in my mind, body, and spirit.

I am centered in truth, happiness, and wisdom.

I am centered with God as my guide.

IS FOR DIFFERENT

Branch Dif•fer•ent (A): Freedom to express yourself without fear of oppression and judgment. Awareness of self. Unique connectedness to everyone else.

Rooted Experience: *Do you fear expressing yourself because of ridicule or judgments from others?*

W orking late hours on warm, beautiful summer nights usually felt tedious and long, especially when the clock in the store ticked like a tortoise.

As I stacked the last roll of receipt paper in the cash register cabinet, I thought about how much I missed working the day shifts, when I used to leave work at 5:00 p.m. with other colleagues.

On a slow and less productive night like that one, there were not many employees around. My commute back to Brooklyn would feel shorter if I had a few more people with me. As I thought of riding home alone, my prayers were answered. Shanta, one of my fun, outgoing, and energetic colleagues, was on her way to Brooklyn that night. She waited for her friend, Kimmy, who worked two blocks away from us.

As we walked toward the train station in the maze of Manhattan's skyscrapers, we gossiped about everything work-related to pass the time away. From the rude customers to some of the demanding managers, every possible topic was up for discussion. With our metro cards in hand, we swiped our way through the turnstiles and strolled down the train station.

"Oh crap, the train is there!" Shanta shouted. Distracted by our juicy gossip, we had not noticed that the Brooklyn-Bridge-bound 6 train had stalled on the upper-level platform.

"Hold it!" we screamed, running down the stairs as fast as we could. All three of us jumped into the first open train car, laughing at the near miss. A genuine and joyous moment of fun and excitement it was for us—until the comments from a disruptive passenger interrupted the flow of our mood.

"It must be fucking Halloween. This must be a joke." Dressed in ripped jeans and a "Brooklyn's Baddest" T-shirt, a young man, sitting two seats away from us, rudely addressed Kimmy, who is transgender. He laughed aloud, trying to grab the attention of the other commuters. However, this was New York, where most people tend to mind their own business.

Appalled by his ignorance, I did not understand why he felt threatened by her looks. Throwing homophobic slurs, he turned toward us in hopes we would engage to create a scene.

"What! You wanna say something?" Shanta and I ignored him. We tried to distract Kimmy from engaging with him as well. But it was too late; his words had already sparked a raging irritation in her glossy brown eyes.

"This fool has no clue." Sitting forward with her arms folded, I could tell she was ready to fight. *What the hell is happening here? Should I say something?* I thought in confusion as I tried to comprehend the unbelievable moment unfolding in front of us.

Shanta and I tried to steer the conversation back to the gossip to lessen the built-up rage in Kimmy's face. Our strategy worked for the guy, since he stopped running his mouth, but not so much for Kimmy, who looked angry and discontented.

After our brief encounter with him, our conversation about our work woes felt disconnected and fake compared to earlier in the night when we had laughed and giggled our retail dramas away. As the train pulled into the Brooklyn Bridge station, an awkwardness in the air stifled our goodbyes. Kimmy's "Safe travels home, my dears" felt abrupt and dry.

From the look in her eyes, I felt this was not her first battle with words of fear and oppression from others. From the look in her eyes, I felt her sadness and anger went deeper than what we had just experienced. From the look in her eyes, I felt her strength in expressing and living in her own truth and freedom. That night, as I showered away the hatred, my eyes filled with tears for her.

I really wish we'd missed that train, I thought, as I dried my swollen eyes. Standing in front of the mirror, a vision of Kimmy's previous encounters with others showing mistreatment and abandonment flashed in front of me. I was unsure of what I was seeing exactly, but there was an immediate connection between her life's story and mine. Her story brought me closer to home, to my own cousin Niko, who was gay and battled living in silence for many years in Jamaica.

Both Kimmy and Niko were born and raised in cultures that shun the idea of their existence. Yet they continued to express their own unique differences, no matter what others did or said about them. I never imagined a night that had started as fun-filled would end up with a bigger picture featuring everyone else. With Shanta's calmness, the young man's ignorance, Kimmy's strength, and Niko's silence, I felt uniquely connected to all of them.

Trunk Insight: *Be Uniquely Different, Yet Understand Your Connection*

To be different means to embrace your true expression of self, not society's perception of how you should behave. It is our own unique personas which make us creative and special. Yet we are not separate or superior to anyone. When we see others from our soul's vantage point, we discover that there are unique ties connecting all of us.

In some way or another, we all have judged or criticized another person or even our own self for being different. Sometimes it's from our own ego's fear and struggle in embracing our true nature. The persons who oppress, discriminate, or judge simply out of hatred, lack their own courage to be themselves, as well. Never tolerate anyone's negativity, but be open to their words—they are teaching you to love yourself and empower you to become in your greatness.

It is possible that they may be inexperienced with a person like you in their surroundings. The fear they try to feed you should only serve as a light in becoming in your power and in embracing your authenticity. There is much self-discovery happening on the forefront of our experiences than we can see.

God created you to glow in your light without fear of what others say about you. There is no need to stay closeted in yourself because of someone else's intolerance. Free yourself from what others have told you about how you should live, dress, or talk. Whatever fears are projected toward you, use as a positive seed to build up the courage to be yourself. If ever you feel that you must adjust yourself for another person to acclimate in an environment, turn three chapters back to the branch of Acceptance.

You were meant to be different for a reason; step forward in your light and become the illuminator in the darkest judgments. You are brave to stand in your truth. You are divinely protected by the light of God. You are loved by all who support you. Allow yourself to be the person you intended to become, without restrictions. Choose to be yourself; it's your divine freedom.

Life is meant to be lived in freedom, not through control or fear based on another person's inability to accept what they do not understand. The freedom to live is to navigate life experiences openly while co-creating with others. The freedom to live is understanding that not everyone will see eye to eye about who you are, but living your life knowing that the power of love rules your heart.

And regardless of what comes on your path—the ridicule, the oppression, the neglect—try to see the bigger picture beyond what's happening in that experience.

We all function as a unit in this ever-changing and at times difficult journey called life. It is a co-creative learning process—which should ideally operate from love, not fear, as we strive for a better future. Will it always be peaceful and happy-go-lucky? Perhaps we may be deluding ourselves or perhaps we can make it work. However, only we can decide which direction we move forward as a society. The more we remain out of alignment because of differences in ideas or belief systems, the more we stay stuck in the cycles of pain, fear, and suffering. Our decision to love wholeheartedly is ours alone to create. At the end of the day, we are all connected to God—the true expression of ourselves.

The difference in you aligns with the difference in me. Through our unique connectedness, we are created to love and be free.

Leaves of Healing: *A Mind Map to Choose Your Own Direction in Life*

Take an honest assessment of your life. Examine the parts of yourself where you feel restricted because of fear of the possible negative feedback you may receive from others. Are you afraid to express who you are? Do you lack the confidence to be yourself because of another person's viewpoint? List one hidden feature you wish you could openly express in your daily life without fear of what anyone thinks. Let's start with the questions below as a guide:

North (N): Which aspect of yourself do you wish to express the most right now?

For example: a hidden talent or skill or a love for something others may deem weird.

East (E): How do you wish to embrace this hidden version more in your life?

West (W): Will embracing this new expression of who you are satisfy you or make you happy in the long-term, and why?

South (S): Are you ready to take this (N), (E), (W) direction regardless of judgments?

Draw a compass on a sheet of paper or in a notebook. Write each answer on its respective compass point in a clockwise direction. Visualize the compass spinning as the winds of change disperse your answers into the roots, planting new seeds of freedom of expression in your reality. Do not be afraid to embrace your hidden side or qualities. Be prepared, because your new direction may serve as shocking news to others but not to your soul.

IS FOR EMPOWER

Branch Em•pow•er (V): Realize your inner strength from your own life's experiences. Use your inner divine power and faith to actualize a better story for yourself.

Rooted Experience: *Where do you get your source of empowerment?*

"Oh! It's Saturday! Where's the remote? I need the remote fast!" My happy seven-year-old-self dived out of bed and dashed for the TV remote before my younger brothers could grab a hold of it.

Before my grandmother went to the food market in downtown Kingston, she had left instructions on a list of household chores to complete prior to her return. Half asleep, I vaguely heard her telling me to "sweep the yard, dust the furniture, and polish the floors" of our small, rented two-bedroom house. However, the only thing I could remember was to watch my favorite cartoon programs as soon as I get out of bed.

I loved cartoons, especially the ones featuring "transforming humans." *Dragon Ball Z*. *The Mighty Morphin Power Rangers*. *He-Man and the Masters of the Universe*. They all possessed magical and mystical powers beaming from the sky to help them fight against evil. I found solace in watching them—since venturing outdoors for fun was never my forte. Out of all of them, *He-Man* was my favorite. I never missed an episode, even though they were only reruns.

He-Man and the Masters of the Universe featured the story of Prince Adam, from the planet of Eternia. He was the protector and keeper of the fantastic secret powers stored away in Castle Grayskull. When Prince Adam's planet faced invasions from the villain Skeletor, he would magically transform into He-Man to save and protect his home world.

Calling forth the power of Grayskull, Prince Adam would wave his mystical sword, affirming, "I have the Power." Amazingly, an unknown lightning force from above the sky illuminated Prince Adam and turned him into the mighty He-Man.

Wow, I wish I was like He-Man, I thought as my eyes glistened in excitement at the shimmering lights emerging from beyond the clouds. The lightning transformation had my butt at the edge of the couch, and I would jump up as if I was receiving that light.

Most times I used my grandmother's broomstick—set aside for cleaning the house—when no one was looking. I pretended to yield my own call to the sky, hoping to be transformed into a powerful avenger.

I wanted to be teleported out of the harsh and confusing reality of the ghetto, where I witnessed women being stabbed by other women over men, men abusing women with machetes, and adults preying on innocent children as scapegoats. I waited, wanted, expected, and needed that light. But nothing happened. *I guess it's not for me.* I felt disappointed each time I tried.

Could it be that I was the villain like Skeletor and did not deserve it? I had already asked God for forgiveness after shaving my brother's head and then running away from home to my aunt's house. Could it be—the stored hatred I held against my environment? Could it be—it was not my time to receive it? Nonetheless, I kept calling out for the light of God, even when "real life" struck me with more darkness and chaos.

As I grew older and life became more complicated, I was slowly giving up because of all the obstacles I endured. The heartbreaks. The emotional and physical abuse. The manipulation by others. The inner rage and discontentment with everything. As much as I tried to "keep the faith" and be calm and patient, my mind recalled the painful reality I lived in.

It gets better; hold onto your inner strength, the guiding inner voice whispered again and again. Yet I disregarded those messages as mere hopes—since life no longer was a cartoon and I no longer felt like becoming He-Man. Then there were times when I felt there was more to this puzzle than what I'd encountered. And each time I was knocked down by storm waves of struggles and obstacles, I would bounce back with a greater sense of resilience and wisdom.

When negativity struck, I recharged with an inner light source of strength, faith, and perseverance. The more I realized my own power, the more I transformed the outer darkness and challenges into a branch of empowerment. All this time I was looking up in the sky for the light to guide me—when the light of God was already illuminated deep within me.

Trunk Insight: *Realize Your Power from Your Struggles*

Every leaf on the Ceiba receives its illuminating source of power from the rays of the sun. It is the light that supplies the leaves with its healing source, just as much as the rain washes away dust and debris. Feeding the Ceiba, the broad leaves nourish the branches, trunk, and roots. As one of the main sources of growth and expansion for the tree, the light flowing through the leaves contributes to the Ceiba's powerful magical state of inner being.

It is the light of God, connected to your higher self, that gives you the power to overcome any obstacle along the way. Every experience, whether good or bad, sprouts a sense of empowerment within, but you must feel it for yourself.

Sometimes, it may feel as if you are in a battle to survive. There are days when life appears more challenging than blissful in nature and everything around you seems convoluted and chaotic. Do not feed any limited beliefs that you cannot move past them. As the difficulties come your way, never allow them to weigh you down into stress and depression. You are more powerful than you realize. See those struggles as a gateway to embrace your true essence.

Every struggle, pain, stress, or turmoil is an opportunity to realize and actualize the power within yourself. Move forward in your faith, with an understanding that you are the master of your experiences. Without faith, it is difficult to feel the change emanating within you. Without faith, all hopes for breakthrough may seem lost and disappointing. Without faith, you may fail to see the light at the end of the tunnel. Tap into your inner power by trusting that all is working out in your favor.

Sometimes we must allow ourselves to fall, only to realize how mightily we bounce back. Every experience has brought you from one point to the next, so release any fears about whether you are strong enough to keep going. Believe your life is changing for the better, even if you are not seeing any results on the horizon. Now is the time to grasp your strength. Call upon God and take inspired movements forward to integrate the powerful inner light in your external reality.

When you come to the realization of your power within, does this mean you should sit back and wait? Absolutely not. Become an agent of transformation by moving forward with clarity and empowerment. Keep going ahead no matter who or what tries to drag you down in the process. Redefine your goals and get clear about what you want. Envision and feel yourself grasping the great opportunities awaiting ahead. Powerful changes illuminate on the horizon—are you ready to embrace them? Feel the light from the Ceiba leaves transforming your struggles into strength.

At the end of a busy and tiring day, make the effort to release any stagnant energy of stress, anxiety, and overwhelm gathered throughout the day. As you stand in your shower or lie in your bath, imagine a waterfall of flaming light pouring over your head. Say the below prayer as the light blazes above and trickles through your entire body. Use this prayer method daily, preferably near a body of water. You can write it down in your phone or a notebook. Read it as often as possible to allow the words to empower you. Prayer is a spiritual gift of encouragement to help you transform your obstacles into triumphs.

Dear God,
I call upon your flaming power and strength to release the negativities holding me back from becoming in my greatness. I place all my worries and fears in this burning light. I know my trials are already transformed into victory and success.

With trust,
[Sign your name here]

IS FOR FORGIVE

Branch For·give (V): Acknowledge the past and free yourself from the painful and hurtful ordeals. Open your mind and heart to release any resentment or anger you have held against yourself and others. Embrace unconditional love to reconnect with God's love and inner peace.

Rooted Experience: *Have you forgiven yourself and them?*

Rain clouds spread across the sky on a refreshing and joyful Sunday morning. There was a warmth and renewed sense of serenity and contentment as my family and I made our way to our church in Queens.

The church itself was small with narrow, lined pews. Each pew seated roughly three to five people, with adequate space to see the front and rear end of the building. Sitting in one of the middle pews—near the pulpit—I smiled brightly with the incoming congregants, being the newly converted member in the congregation.

At sixteen years old, I took a dip in the holy water in hopes for "redemption of my sins" as the pastors defined the transformation process. Despite my fear of drowning, I decided to take this avenue for my own spiritual pursuit in finding harmony in my mind and becoming closer to God. *If only I could wash all the pains and struggles away. This has to be the way.* I hoped and prayed for absolution before taking the plunge. Yet deep within I still struggled in confusion about my life after the "cleansing."

"Please be seated, everyone. We are about to commence the service." Sister Pauline, the church's events coordinator, stood tall in her large purple hat, which sprouted peacock-like feathers. She knocked on the mic once again, calling for everyone's attention.

As everyone was seated, she flipped through the pages of her notebook and began to read the schedule of events for the upcoming month of June. She spoke with poise but read the announcements briskly while watching the clock mounted between the two large majestic side pillars. Giving her closing remarks to progress the service forward, she called on all new visitors to stand and introduce themselves.

The first visitor, dressed in dark-colored jeans and a red T-shirt, stood up a few benches away from me.

"Hi, I'm John from Queens," he said softly.

The second visitor, seated in front of me, gave her introduction with strong praise and worship.

"Hello church! Amen! I said amen, church! I am here with Sister Susie." She rocked side to side infused with a blast of energy, and then sat down abruptly, while her body danced back and forth.

Assuming that was the last of the welcomes, I turned to face the announcer. But a final newcomer, sitting at the rear end of the church, had yet to state his name and where he was from.

"Hello, I'm…" He stood up shyly. Before he finished his name and introduction, the familiarity of his face and voice rung stress into my heart.

What the—? A raging storm developed within when I saw him. The new visitor, who was also a former friend of my family, blasted me into the past—to my earlier childhood years in Jamaica.

My childhood years were quite eventful. There were moments of cheerfulness and laughter, as well as moments of broken innocence from harrowing experiences. I struggled to suppress the horrendous flashbacks of being raped and sexually abused as a child.

Although years had passed, the mental hauntings were non-stop, wreaking hatred and despair silently within me.

The first encounter began at five years old, when I was repeatedly molested by the teenage son of my then-babysitter. He did what he wanted while his mother went out grocery shopping. I never understood what was happening or why he threatened to stifle me with a pillow if I talked.

"If you talk, Mi will kill yuh and yuh grandmother." I did as I was told.

Fast forward to age seven. I tried to block out a horrendous experience after being sexually abused by a group of teenage boys in my housing unit. They had their "fun" with me while the adults were not around. Feeling unclean and ashamed, I begged God for answers and mercy from the cruelty of my reality. But nothing changed, and my life took a turn for the worse.

Fourteen years and rebellious, I was angry and out of control. That time around, the raging fire developing within my heart destroyed another sexual advance with the Mr. New-Visitor-in-My-Church. He tried but never got any further than the forceful nature of my fists. What he had not realized was that I was already drenched with bitterness from my earlier encounters. Not only was I furious at him, but I never forgave or trusted anyone again—not even my own self.

And there he was, smiling from ear to ear. He stood dapper in a smooth brown suit awaiting a warm welcome in my safe haven. The one who tried and lost. The one whose face I prayed I would never see again. The one whom I begged God to deliver justice and judgment upon.

How is this justice, my God? I sobbed within.

Justice did not feel great—not one bit.

"I can't believe he's here," I said aloud in disbelief, not realizing that Susan, a fellow church sister, sat next to me.

"What do you mean?" she questioned in confusion. She looked surprised by the awestruck expression in my eyes.

"Someone I used to, um—to know, um…" I stumbled on how to respond to her. I knew she wanted to know more by the way she tapped me on my shoulder. However, my mind was already far gone into a world of distress and questions.

Is this a sick joke? How in heaven's name did he come to find this small church? What the hell is this? I wanted answers but only heard and felt the pains of the past resurfacing. The stressful pressure of the moment pulsated through my veins. All the suppressed hurt boiled over my body like hot lava. The world suddenly felt smaller as my wounds reopened. Then our eyes met from a distance, causing his confident smile to quake in a shocking frown.

As the sermon progressed, my attention strayed away from the inspirational messages I often look forward to and into the abyss of past events, replaying all the physical and sexual abuse. As I sat there, a teardrop attempted to force itself onto my face, but I held strong with pride, not wanting anyone to see me this way.

Forgive and let go, an inner voice whispered, but only one other *F* word played repeatedly. There was a developing fire burning within me, one that I could not control. Yet there was also a calming force holding my arms—whispering, *It's ok, my dear. Let it all go.*

The sermon reached its end, and Pastor Jones called on anyone in need of prayer and God's saving grace. I had considered going for prayer but changed my mind when I saw my attacker walking sadly to the altar with tears streaming down his face.

Nonsense! My mind judged his emotions as lies and deceit, but deep within I felt sorry for him as much as I did for myself. I wanted to escape the church immediately but was frozen in my tracks as he headed in my direction.

Where is he going? Please don't come my way. The tension increased as I held my fears and tears at bay. He approached me with his head lowered in shame, and as he wiped his tears and snot away.

"Hi. Umm…I'm truly sorry for everything I did to you."

Standing in silence, I was uncertain what to say or whether I should acknowledge his apology. *What! You are sorry? Is this hap-*

pening? My ego was not allowing this, but my soul took charge and answered in calmness.

"It's okay. I am good." Shocked at myself, I could not believe I had given him such a simple response. Everything I once knew as truth tumbled to the ground. My faith. My strength. My every ounce of existence.

That evening, the world around caved in on me as I cried a Nile at home. Life felt unreal and my body was numbed to the bone. I did not understand what I did to deserve such torture. I felt foolish in having assumed that peace would come easy and thinking that the church itself would grant me ultimate deliverance. Never did I imagined that justice involved facing my own dark shadows.

However, in truth, a brief sense of hope engulfed my heart after accepting his apology. My heart also slightly opened with a light, regardless of what had transpired that day. My soul held strong to the belief that one day my life would make sense through all the madness. There was a surety that I would find the clarity I sought, but only through compassion and unconditional love.

Over the years, as I learned to let go of my own resentments, guilt, and regret attached to those experiences, slowly but surely, I embraced the power, courage, and strength to forgive myself and the men who raped me. A choice I made for my own inner peace and happiness.

Trunk Insight: *Let Go: Forgive Yourself and Them*

Forgiving yourself and others is one of the key branches to unlock your inner Ceiba. But is it ever easy to forgive someone for the pain and suffering you endured from their words or actions? Is it ever easy to let go when the painful memories keep replaying or resurfacing? Is it ever easy to come face to face with your own demons? No one ever said the path of forgiveness would be a walk in the park. Nonetheless, it is a necessary climb to return to the true love of God within yourself.

Before you forgive another person for the pain they may have caused, you must, first and foremost, forgive yourself and let go of those hurtful emotional experiences you've held onto.

Forgiveness is a powerful branch to heal yourself in order to embrace the love you deserve. Forgiveness is not dwelling on the guilt and shame you felt as a result of another person's behavior. Forgiveness is not feeding on the negative memories of what others have done to you in hopes for retribution. It is not a redoing of an experience because you wished it did not happen. It is an expansion and growth to incorporate inner peace and freedom in all areas of your life. Feel into your heart and allow love to lead the way without attachment to the pain or suffering of an ordeal.

However, the inconvenient truth is that, as much as we may try to let go of past hurt, abuse, or neglect, forgiving ourselves is one of the hardest tests we face as souls in this lifetime. Letting go of resentments and anger include uprooting, reevaluating, and facing those unwanted memories we have disregarded over a period of time. These painful experiences can trigger immense anger if we have not made peace with the past. The emotional reactions are not meant to hurt you or keep you stuck. They can help you unlock the portal of love in your heart that has been sealed by bitterness and hatred. The path of forgiveness will lead you toward profound healing and transformation if you allow yourself to "let go and let God" do the work.

The Creator knows that you were wronged by others, but holding onto to the blame only hurts yourself. It's for your own benefit that you let go of any grudges. To do that, search inwards for clarity and strength to move forward from the experience. The answers are within you. As much as you search outside of yourself for peace in a situation, know that true serenity occurs when you deepen your connection to God. It is never worth investing your energy in misery about what others have done. Free yourself from the emotional trauma, because you deserve utmost joy and happiness in your journey.

Release the pains of the past by accepting and reconnecting with the truth of who you are. You are a powerful being of love and compassion. Realize your inner power to accept, heal, and love yourself without conditions. Release your blames, resentments, and hurt by giving your tears and fear to God. Open your heart to receive the divine embrace of harmony that is long overdue in your life. The painful emotions you've held onto are not feeding you freedom but holding you back from living in true happiness. The powerful branch of Forgiveness wants you to take back your divine right to live from a place of unconditional love. Let go by forgiving yourself and the people who have betrayed, harmed, or hurt you in any form. Trust in the power of God to handle the situation for you.

Leaves of Healing: *Ho'oponopono Mantra*

One of the most powerful affirmations that can assist with resolving emotional traumas and pain in relationships is a Hawaiian mantra called Ho'oponopono. The Hawaiian word pono loosely translates to "righteousness" and is used as a healing word to attain balance and peace in one's relationships. The mantra can be used to resolve unhealed issues with a partner, a family member, a friend, or even yourself. It begins "I love you. I am sorry. Please forgive me. I thank you." Like any invocation, you must have pure intent before you incorporate these words as a guide. Uttering the mantra emits a powerful, healing vibration of compassion and love. Open your heart and mind to the beautiful flow of these simple yet powerful words to assist in forgiving yourself and others.

Close your eyes. Visualize yourself standing at the base of the tall, majestic Ceiba tree as the sun beams through its leaves. In the distance, you notice a person walking towards you. It could be a person you want to forgive or even your own self. They are now facing you and asking for your forgiveness as well. Place your right palm on the tree, as the other person does the same. Place your left hand onto their heart as they also do the same with you. To begin, breathe in love, trust, and acceptance, and breathe out resentments, hurt, and blame. Allow the divine loving energy from the Ceiba's trunk to flow into your heart and into their heart. Now gently say the mantra:

I'm sorry.
Please forgive me.
I thank you.
I love you.

[Do this exercise three times before you get out of bed each day for at least twenty-six days.]

G

IS FOR GRATEFUL

Branch Grate·ful (A): Satisfied with what you already have in the present moment. Appreciative of life in its simplicity. Thankful to God for everyone and everything.

> **Rooted Experience:** *Are you more grateful or more complaining each day?*

As the new kid on the block in an American high school, I had to navigate through the culture shock of switching outfits every single school day. Before I migrated to America, my high school fashion trend entailed colorful dress tunics and polished black shoes back in Jamaica. Overall, I cared little about how I dressed or what I wore. However, to acclimate to my new environment, an adjustment in my wardrobe was necessary. But adhering to this new way of life was not easy for a teenage girl, especially when my outfits were bland and limited to what my father could afford.

"I like your sneakers. Are those classic low-tops?" Juan examined my size-nine feet. He was also new to the school and was a fashion trend-setter who wore smooth Sean John jackets and Ecko Red jeans. Dropping his muscular sixteen-year-old body into the desk next to me, he smiled for a response.

"Umm, yeah. They are Nikes." I blushed while he perused them. *Duh, Terry! Everyone knows that.* I gulped in embarrassment at my response—even more so remembering the small hole peeping at the back of my sneakers.

"Yeah, I know," he giggled.

"I used to have a red-and-white one before I bought these Jordans."

I crossed my legs to hide the wear and tear, while he showcased his trendy new black-and-white Michael Jordan "Bunnies," as they called them. Almost every kid in school was wearing them.

The Bunnies sneakers were very sleek, clean, and unusual, but I knew I couldn't afford them. From what I overheard from the other kids, who bragged to their friends, the cost of a new pair of Air Jordans—depending on the model—ranged between $100.00 and $150.00. They looked exquisite, and my cheap low-tops, which cost forty bucks, were nothing compared to them.

"Oh, very nice." I admired the intriguing designs on the edge of the sole, as well as his beautiful hazel eyes staring back at me.

"Thanks, cutie." He smiled and refocused his attention to the blackboard, where Ms. Pena welcomed the new and returning sophomores in her second-level Spanish course.

As I sat in class, I could not concentrate on the lesson. I was busy surveying and tallying the number of kids who wore at least some version of an Air Jordan. *I want some*, I thought and wished in desperation, even though I knew that money was limited.

As an immigrant in a new land, my father could barely afford to buy me new clothing and shoes on a regular basis. At home, the closet I shared with my cousins housed three pairs of sneakers for myself. However, most days I wore the same pair of blue-and-white Nikes, since the other pairs were some no-name brands I had purchased at a thrift store. I was determined to buy a pair of Air Jordans, among many other things, no matter the cost.

That night, I stared at my bedroom ceiling, fantasizing about buying loads of new Air Jordans, some gold hoop earrings, and a few gold necklaces with my name engraved on them. I also wanted a cute pink Wilson's leather jacket like the one I had seen a girl wear in chemistry class. *Geez, I wish I had my own money to buy myself some decent clothes and shoes.*

Positioning myself to sleep, I frowned at my poor, miserable life. I questioned God as to why I struggled as a hard-working student while the other kids who walked the hallways daily had everything they wanted. Basking in the moonlight glow beaming through my window pane, I grew tired from all my fussing and drifted off into the astral planes.

While I wished my dreams manifested some fancy, luxurious items that night, instead I envisioned myself running in the empty hallway of my high school. I strolled through the cold, eerie, and desolate hallways as a parade of dark shadows descended from the walls and chased after me. Petrified, I ran into a nearby classroom, which abruptly transformed into my bedroom. As I lay outstretched on my back, the air felt strained as my breath slowly parted from my partially awakened body.

Oh God, they got me!

I muffled a scream while I tried to break free from the nightmare restraints. Then I began to mumble Psalm 23 from the Bible—a tip I recalled from my Jamaican upbringing to ward off demons. *The Lord is my Shepherd, I shall not want*—I repeated on and on. But the holds of the nightmare felt more powerful than my words. Gasping for air, I finally broke free from the horrific restraints. The sweat from my back ran profusely down into my nightgown as if I had just run a marathon.

The next day, episodes of that terrible nightmare replayed in my thoughts. But I ignored them. My attention was solely focused on the weekly allowance I was to collect from my father on Saturday mornings. I prayed he would have enough money for me so I could buy my new pair of Air Jordans.

"I'll see if I can get some more money to you next week." Disappointed and annoyed, I stood face to face with him in front of the sneaker store.

"Okaay. I really wanted more today."

"I said I'll see what I can do next week."

"But I wanted to buy the sneakers now so I can wear them to school on Monday."

He pushed back. As he looked at me in disappointment, the dream resurfaced once again. While I complained in my mind, I also noticed the heavy bags under his eyes, illustrating fine lines of frustration and stress. There was an uncanny feeling that he was financially struggling to care for himself. And, on repeat, the scriptures replayed like a broken record in my head: *I shall not want. I shall not want. I shall not want.*

An epiphany slapped me awake as I stared at my father's worn out face. I realized that I had everything made out for me but remained in constant complaint. Because I wanted to fulfill my own desires, I had become extremely ungrateful and selfish in the process. I had a solid roof over my head, not the patched-up rooftop back in Jamaica. I had free access to education, not the school fee my grandmother usually struggled to pay every school term. Instead of appreciating what God had already blessed me with, I was fussing over "Bunnies." My own complaints created an unnecessary nightmare for me to face my own pride and address how unappreciative I was becoming with my new life in America.

Trunk Insight: *Be More Grateful Every Day*

The nice house. The nice car. The dream job. We all visualize, dream, or sometimes obsess about these things. However, at times, we tend to forget how important it is to give thanks for the simple things of life. The free-flowing air we breathe. The people around us. Mother Earth's nurturing grace and wonder.

There is no shame in wanting or acquiring the material things of the world. But if we complain about what we do not have, then we only create more unwanted stress and misery for ourselves. If we focus on what we cannot have with impatience, then our own complaints can take a toll on our mind, body, and soul. Is it worth the unnecessary overthinking, stress, or anxiety about what's not happening right now? If we continually feed the "I don't have this or that" thoughts, we will only feed more stagnation and blockage in our abundance. To free ourselves from our own worries, we must adjust our focus away from the lack and toward the embrace of the simple appreciations of life in the here and now.

Each moment we focus on what's not working in our lives, we attract more of the same experiences. If the lines are too long at the supermarket and we complain, then each time we visit the store the line will appear twice as long as before. If your supervisor doesn't give you the desired recognition for a job well done, and you complain, then the you'll feel less appreciation, even when you did your best. If your plans seem to be falling apart, the more you complain, the more everything around you will appear to be cursed or going haywire. To experience a better reality— and reduce unnecessary worries—be more grateful for what you have now rather than complaining about what is not available to you yet. Constant complaints only block the physical manifestations of your dreams and wishes.

The Universe is a mirror which only reflects back what we focus our attention toward. When we fuel negative thoughts, we re-enforce that reality to a greater magnitude. When we express appreciation, we flow more easily in patience and understanding. God will supply what we ask for if we put much focus on what we want in a state of gratitude. You have food on the table. You have a job to pay your bills. You can read and write your name. Make the effort to feel good each day by tipping the scale of worries toward more appreciation of life itself. Here are a few simple appreciations to remind you of how blessed you are:

Simple Appreciations of Life

Appreciate who you are, first and foremost. You are a beautiful soul who can manifest what you want if you release your complaining and start living from your soul. Be grateful for yourself and realize that the true splendors of joy, peace, and love continuously surround you.

Appreciate your mind for what it is. It is a powerful instrument, with the ability to create your desired reality with clear focus and productive thinking. It is a resourceful tool to utilize wisely every day. Give it rest by delving into prayer or meditation. When you feed your mind with positive thoughts and affirmations, you're fueling its potential to create better experiences. Appreciate your beautiful mind, for it is the keeper of incredible unexplored talents and gifts.

Appreciate your ego for what it is. The controller and unconscious defender. The comfort-zone creator and survivor. Your ego can assist you in moving forward when it's attuned to your highest potential. It is an intelligent tool of your mind, so give it more meaningful roles to play in your life. While the ego has been the source of many complaints and worries, the trouble only occurs when you allow your ego to roam wildly in your mental forest. Recognize its power in attaining success, as long as it is used wisely as an element of change. Recognize the times when your ego became selfish to save you from being used by others. Recognize the ego's impact at times when you feared to make a change in your lifestyle, and then it pushed you into adverse situations to teach you a lesson. Be grateful for the power of this divine part of yourself, because it is essential for elevating you beyond what you've outgrown. Make your ego your friend and not your controller.

Appreciate your body for what it is. It is your perfectly structured vessel of divine essence emanating in majesty and beauty. You must take care of your body and nourish it with healthy food and exercise. It is a vehicle of movement when change presents itself. It has many talents and attributes when used appropriately and respectfully. It is an acting agent, always ready to take the next steps with you when you are ready. The more you nourish your body with a healthy lifestyle, the better it works as a force of willpower toward manifesting your dream life.

Appreciate everyone around you. Whether at work, school, or home, every person plays a unique role in your soul's evolutionary process. The person who told you you are unworthy assists you in shining your truth and becoming the best version of yourself. The person who showered you in compliments helps you to see your own self-worth and build your self-confidence. The person who belittled you assists you to reconnect with your inner strength and power to transcend judgments. Appreciate those people for who they are— they contribute to your internal expansion and growth. After all, we are collectively joined as ONE in connection to God despite our visible differences.

Appreciate every present moment as much as you can. Your attitude toward each day plays a vital role in how you feel. Every day is a new day given to you—be thankful for life. The beautiful glistening sun. The raindrops on your window pane. The playful birds whistling melodies. The free air we breathe of Mother Nature. They all allow us to delight in the splendid beauty of life— regardless if the rain clouds darken our hopes or the sun brightens our smile. As we infuse ourselves in the glory of love and nature, we reconnect with the true essence of who we are as powerful creators. And in honor of the simple appreciations of life, let us aim to create more grateful days going forward.

Leaves of Healing: *The Branches Toward Gratitude Affirmations*

Rest your eyes for a minute or two before turning to the next chapter. Use this very moment to smile, inhale deep, and appreciate the air engulfed around you. Exhale a deep breath to release any recent complaints you've been feeding to yourself. Doesn't it feel good? To breathe and feel yourself flowing in the present moment? Repeat the below affirmations to yourself (out loud or in your mind). Feel the shift in your energy as the first seven branches of affirmation in your inner Ceiba permeate your mind, body, and soul.

I ACCEPT who I am and change what I can.

I am BEAUTIFUL both inside and out.

I am CENTERED in my mind, body, and spirit.

I am DIFFERENT and connected to everyone around me.

I EMPOWER myself to live in my truth.

I FORGIVE myself and others as I heal my inner wounds.

*I am GRATEFUL for everything and allow my blessings
to enter my life.*

IS FOR HONEST

Branch Hon•est (A): True to yourself. Living your life without trying to validate yourself to anyone.

Rooted Experience: *Are you compromising your integrity for others?*

Occasionally, a few coworkers would invite me to go clubbing with them on the weekends, but I would kindly decline the offers. Aside from the usual family gatherings in a summer-ready backyard plush with a swimming pool and a barbecue grill, nightclubs were not my cup of tea. I was a laid-back type of girl who enjoyed reading poems, traveling to distant countries, and spending time alone. As far as clubbing was concern, it was the least activity on my list of fun things to consider.

"How can you be Jamaican and not party? You got to be Jah-fakin'." Brian, the resident comedic coworker, poked jokes at me in the work lunchroom. The comments arose after I had declined another offer to attend our coworker Susan's birthday celebration at Club Taboo in Brooklyn.

"I cannot imagine you being at a club. You are like a goodie type." He continued his jokes. With his long, slender hands, he arose from his chair, and marched out of the lunchroom to return to his duties.

The nerve of him! What is he trying to say? I'm boring? I smiled to mask my annoyance at his statements. *Oh, please! I can be fun! I can definitely get down.* I was exasperated and embarrassed after feeling devoured on the break-room discussion plate. To prove him wrong, I changed my usual weekend plans of doing nothing and accepted Susan's invitation—knowing very well he would be there.

As the weekend approached, a barrage of questions overflowed in my mind. It was my first experience partying with my coworkers, and I was a nervous wreck. *Damn, what are you doing?* I checked my itsy-bitsy black mini-dress in the mirror and wobbled along my bedroom carpet in my five-inch purple stilettos. While doing my hair and makeup I wondered how the night would unfold.

From what I had overheard through eavesdropping on the many stories told by party-going coworkers, some Brooklyn clubs seemed wild and unruly even with the bouncers around. I knew I was in over my head on this one. In all honesty, I was unsure how to act and could not help but to feel disconnected from who I was.

Spending money I did not have on clothing and shoes, for one night only, became one of the questionable feelings, among other things. As a college student who depended on financial aid and an eight dollar-per-hour retail job, I could barely afford to pay my regular bills. Not only did I sigh at my low, almost depleted bank account balance, but I also cringed at the angels and demons who were drinking tea on my shoulders.

It's a party! Suck it up! the inner demon chimed in to persuade me to stop caring about my financial woes and buy whatever I wanted. Yet somehow I felt I was only spending money to impress people who I may never see again.

Are you sure about this? the inner angel interjected. But I checked the mirror once more and twirled in awe at how sexy I looked. With a proud smirk, I imagined Brian's face drooping on the dance floor, as well as the number of heads I planned to turn in that dress.

Halfway inside the club, lines of people stood with wristbands waiting to be checked in.

"Heyyy! Tracy, right?" I recognized the face of a coworker. I had no idea of his name and, based on his question, it turns out that he did not know mine.

"It's Terry!" I shouted above the music beating through the walls.

Eyeing me up and down, he said, "Wow, you look great." He appeared shocked to see me here, but my focus was set on finding Susan—and on seeing Brian's reaction.

As I entered the club, I peeped over the crowd of people, but Susan was nowhere in sight. Everyone was high on excitement. People danced and sang the latest dance hall tunes. An overwhelming feeling of anxiety surged within me from the parade of noise.

Meandering through the tight mass, I found a happy Susan jumping up and down in the VIP section.

"Terry! So glad you could make it. You look awesome!" She was ecstatic as she danced on a small table filled with ice buckets of liquor.

"Everyone, this is Terry!" She gave a woozy introduction to a table of a few familiar faces from work and other unknown people. *What the hell are you doing here, Terry?* I asked myself. *Stop it! Enjoy the moment.* I caught my erratic emotions.

As the night progressed into the wee hours of the morning, my physical body could not withstand the pain of the stilettos rubbing against my heels. Numbed from being planted in the same spot all night, I barely felt my big toes.

"Hi. Would you like to dance, pretty girl?" A handsome-looking guy approached me.

"Umm, no, I'm good." I smiled, pretending not to feel the burn in my feet.

"Don't be shy. I won't step on your toes." He said. *Damn is it that obvious?* I laughed at myself. Watching Susan having fun made me wonder, *Why not enjoy the moment as well?* The night was still young and alive, and so it would not hurt to dance the pain off with him.

Oh Lord Jesus, he is sexy, I thought as we slow danced to Usher's "U Got it Bad." Later that morning, I found myself sipping pineapple juice with a tip of vodka—not remembering I did not drink alcohol. I made every minute count, although I felt conflicted about what I was doing.

At 6:00 a.m., the sun beamed against the neon-lit club sign, *Taboo*, as I walked wearily out of a dark room. Exhausted from a night of partying, I had enjoyed the last few hours.

Wait a minute. The moment hit me. I realized that I hadn't seen Brian. He had never shown up and was nowhere in sight—after all the effort I put into looking my best.

Why am I here, again? I questioned my reasoning and decision. I was disappointed that Brian never caught a glimpse of me being spontaneous for a change. *Oh well. It happened already,* I thought, unapologetic for my brief night in the club. However, I felt guilty that I deceived and compromised my own self just to prove a point.

Foolishly, I had sought some validation from him instead of being honest about who I was. Laughing, not from the vodka but from the self-realization of the moment, I could not believe that it took someone else's opinion to enjoy a night-out in the town instead of naturally going on my own accord.

Trunk Insight: *Stay True for Yourself, Not for Anyone Else*

One of the most important branches in your inner Ceiba is being honest about who you are. Honesty is a battle many of us fight within, especially when we partake in "questionable" experiences that we know are out of alignment with our truth. When you engage in an experience, whether it is a new romance, a new career path, or a buying decision, always ask yourself "Am I doing it because I want to, or is it to please someone else?"

We all have lived in some version of ourselves where we had to adjust our persona to acclimate to a certain environment. And whatever the reasons may be, do not judge or feel guilty about it.

Experiencing life outside of our comfort zone is all part of the learning curve to reconnect with the truth of who we are becoming. Every rooted experience serves as a lesson for growth and for us to understand more about our true nature. Your encounters, whether you consider them good or bad, allow you to weed out the wants and the do-not-wants as you gradually progress forward on your life's path.

How can we know what is for us if we have not experienced some contrast in the process? Life is not about going fishing for trouble to test our limits but involves finding ourselves sometimes in the most vulnerable and uncomfortable situations. Yet we must not judge the encounters but observe and allow those moments to occur without control or expectation. We must try to reap the wisdom in the lessons to either integrate the experience or change what does not align to our soul's truth. These experiences are not only meant to teach us but also to prepare us for more "questionable" paths along the way.

We must experience life in order to grasp the insights we need to expand as souls. As much as we try to avoid engaging in certain activities or events, they can be difficult to outrun. Your soul chooses a path for you in order to take away the wisdom, if you allow yourself to see the bigger picture at hand. Do not blame yourself if you have deviated from what you are used to once in a while.

Sometimes your soul is also trying to highlight some aspects of a deep-rooted personality in your unconscious mind that you might have been unaware of. Then again, you always have the power of choice at your grasp before you decide to engage in any activity—use discernment. Only you will know what is for you as you grasp the wisdom, knowledge, and lessons an experience is showing.

Observe your emotional reactions as you move through life and interact with others. Does an experience make you feel good, or does it make you feel disconnected or uncomfortable? Never go against your inner knowing if a path does not serve your highest good. Follow your heart and use your mind wisely. Reevaluate your actions and behavior if you want to create a different story. Wherever you are or whatever you do in life, know that there is no need to compromise your integrity or dignity for anyone's gain or pleasure.

There is no need to force yourself into an environment for the good will of others. If ever you feel you have to prove yourself to another person, take a step back and ask, "Am I expressing the sincere truth about myself?" You are the pollinator of your experiences. You decide if you want to bloom better moments or keep fueling the opinions that another person projects at you. Once you remain true to who you are, God shines a guiding light on the ones who will stand by your side.

As you realign to your authentic self, in due time you will attract the people or events that flow more with your soul. You are the only person responsible for your own path of creation toward happiness. Ensure what you express in your life is your truth and nothing less than that. Being honest does not require approval from anyone. Being honest liberates your soul, while pretense only stagnates your mind. Being honest requires no validation but the confidence and courage to be your true divine self.

Leaves of Healing: *True Self-Reflective Questions and Answers*

Take your right index fingers and use it to make a swirling figure eight around your heart. The eight sign represents an infinite loop of connection to your true self and a reminder that you are never disconnected, regardless of where you are or what you are doing. Now answer the following questions and do not hold back with the answers. Allow them to flow from the truth of your soul.

a. *Do I ever compromise myself in any experience, and why?*
   For example, think of a party, on the train, in traffic,
   at work, at the café, or even in a family gathering.

b. *What can I do to remain connected to my true self?* For example, you may use an exercise such as the affirmation, "I am honest about who I am"; music that you enjoy—Michael Jackson's *Invincible* album; or the looping eight exercise above.

c. *Will I remember to stay true to who I am while I create my new life?* For example, you can remind yourself, "I may stray for a while, but I will always return to my truth with no regrets or shame, and with God as my guidance."

IS FOR INTUITIVE

Branch In·tu·i·tive (A): Knowing inwardly. Using your inner guidance tool to navigate life alongside your logical mind.

Rooted Experience: *Which do you use often: intuition, ego, or both?*

It was approaching the end of my work shift at Target, and sleeping was the main priority on my midnight agenda. It had been a busy evening at work with last-minute customers and cleanups at the cash registers, and I felt anxious to catch the final bus heading to East New York.

The bus terminal was about seven to ten minutes away from the store, which was in the middle of the gigantic, open Gateway shopping mall. Looking at my watch, I paced the time when the B13 bus, the most convenient ride I needed, was expected to depart.

Catching that bus at night was a nuisance. Sometimes it didn't matter how fast I ran, I still often missed my rides. Usually, the driver could hardly see anyone coming from their vantage point.

"I'm not missing that bus," I proudly told myself as I closed my locker and headed out the store. Walking briskly through the empty parking lot, I checked to see if anyone from Home Depot or Staples was around. There were no signs of life but the cloudy sky above, which sparked a hazy mist with mysterious edginess. Five minutes away from the terminal, I received a phone call from Maria, a childhood friend, I had not heard from in years.

It's too late to talk to anyone. An annoyance brewed from the lateness of the ring. My mind was set on one goal and one goal only—to be on that bus by 11:05 p.m. Any conversation would only distract or slow me down.

"Hey, what's up, Maria?" An eagerness within pushed me to answer all the same.

"How are you doing, Terry? It's been a long time," she replied.

"I thought about you and wanted to check in on you."

Her soft and calm angelic voice helped relax my anxious catch-that-bus mind and ease the work tension in my tired shoulders. Yet, for other reasons, her voice alerted an unusual feeling. *Why would she phone me at this hour of the night?* I asked myself as she chatted on the other end of the line. But I disregarded that first thought: *It's nothing.* I listened to her reminisce on our old teenage years. While she carried the conversation back into crazy memories, my eyes tuned into another "distraction" quickly developing in the parking lot.

At the corner of my eyes, I spotted two short, muscular male figures emerging from a white parked, unmarked commercial van. They glanced at each other and signaled a peculiar hand gesture like birds flapping wings. My eyes may have deceived me, but my inner guidance sensed something was off. Like a harpy eagle protecting its young from the monkeys in the Ceiba, I watched them cautiously as they walked in my direction.

Suddenly, one of the men quickened his steps toward the front of me, while the other, barely visible, circled to the back of me. Brisk but cautious in movement, they walked with a sense of urgency. I pretended not to notice, engaging more in the phone conversation, but deep within I felt these men were more than package delivery drivers—since their hands were empty.

Damn, this does not look good. They increased their pace. Calm in posture but nervous, I fought in my mind whether to start running toward the bus terminal—not to abort the plan—or to turn back to the store where more people were.

Turn back! Turn back! Run! an inner voice shouted. But my mind was still set on catching that bus. *Dammit!* Before I could say "hold on" to Maria, who was still talking on the phone, I sprinted toward the store as if I was running the hundred-meters dash against Usain Bolt.

Panting heavily, I arrived at the front of the store and glanced around to see if they were chasing me, but instead they jumped in their van and sped off immediately. I guessed they had never expected my speed or knew that I was onto their insidious scheme. Their plans were foiled, but I had missed my ride.

As I sat in another bus, the unintended ride of the night, I thought of all the what ifs and maybes of the possible outcomes if I had gone against my intuition. I felt that, if I had run toward the bus stop, they would have intercepted me regardless of how close I was. Turning back seemed less logical to my ego, and yet following my intuition had prevented the worst that could have happened. I was most grateful for answering the call from Maria, my unbeknownst guardian angel, who had sparked an inner knowing that something was wrong.

Trunk Insight: *Let Your Intuition Lead and Put Your Ego on Call*

Every person has been blessed with intuitive abilities and gifts. That inner knowing without evidence or need for confirmation. That inner compass or guidance system. That tightening feeling in our stomach. At the same time, everyone has also been blessed with their own unique human identity—the ego. The bearer of comfort zones, and other times the instiller of fear or pride to push us into survival mode. Our intuition and ego are divine tools, granted by God, that we must use to navigate our journey. Yet, what roles have you consciously assigned to each intelligence in your life?

Call upon your ego, when necessary.

The ego carries a bad reputation for initiating the controlling and impulsive nature of ourselves. There is nothing wrong with the ego. We need to use it when we can. The problem is, we often give it more power to create our experiences than our own intuition. It is unfortunate that it has become the source of a myriad of problems.

We should never disregard the existence of this natural part of our intelligence or discount its role as a teacher of lessons, an agent of change, or, most importantly, a protector from danger. Yet, if we allow our ego to run wildly in our lives, asking a list of unnecessary questions or preventing us from taking inspired action, then it will lead us astray.

Remember, you are a powerful creator with the ability to re-evaluate and renew your ego's role. This means that when the times get tough and the tough sees no other exits, you can call upon your ego to be the agent of change when needed. Make the conscious effort to be the director of your experiences. Start by changing your ego's full-time contract from creating your experiences to becoming an on-call agent of changing desperate and life-altering situations.

To escape a toxic or abusive relationship, use your ego's selfish nature to move on with your life with less consideration of what anyone thinks. It is looking out for your own best interest, betterment, and happiness. If you have reached the breaking point in your career, use your ego's no-more-settling ways to advance toward other career opportunities that expand your professional growth. If you are being taken advantage of by another person, use your ego wisely to safely clear them from your space or set healthy boundaries between you and them. Allow your ego to be the agent of needed changes and movements, minus any fear or impulsive action. You can produce positive outcomes with your ego when it collaborates effectively with your intuitive self in the lead.

Put your intuition in the lead always.

Our intuitive nature knows without logical reasoning and assists us in seeing the bigger picture that our ego tends to dismiss. As we use our intuitive self, there is a better understanding without the rational need for evidence or confirmation. That inner spark will ignite a feeling that something feels either right or wrong.

In all that you do, follow your intuition. Allow it—not your ego—to be the creative tool in charge. There are no unnecessary questions or second-guessing when you have tapped into this divine power within yourself. Sometimes the negative aspects of your ego may want to intrude. But you know you have the power of free will to overrule its opposition. At any given moment when fears or limitations arise, follow the call of your heart and soul, and use discernment to make wise decisions that work best for personal growth.

Sometimes, there is a thin line between intuitive knowing and ego-based action. To differentiate between the two, trust your first thought—the one that feels certain beyond a reasonable doubt. You will know when the moment is right when a decision or an idea evokes feelings of excitement and joy, not confusion or dismay. And, if ever you feel uncertain about who is leading the path forward, take a step back and allow yourself to feel into the moment.

Not every direction will make sense, but always follow that inner knowing, bridging the connection between your heart and soul. Remain confident that the path you have chosen is aligned to your soul's expansion and for your highest good. Your intuitive nature is the source of all creative pursuits. And the more you utilize this divine, intelligent tool in your experiences, the better you navigate different circumstances with ease and flow. Remember that you are the creator of your own story. You can manifest your dreams using your intuitive self in the lead while your ego nature waits on call.

Leaves of Healing: *A Memo to the Ego*

Allow your intuitive nature to be the driver while you take your ego along for the ride to traverse the tests of life. To assist you in realigning your ego's contract, I want you to send it a memo every week (any day you decide) to thank it for its "creative" service fueled with lessons and to remind it of its new role and mission in your life's experiences.

Date: Now
Effective: Immediately
RE: Reassignment of Life CONTRACT

Dear Agent Ego,
It is with deep happiness and content that I'm informing you that you have been re-assigned to a new mission in my life. Forever-more, I will call upon you only when drastic changes are needed. I know this is hard for you to hear, since you are used to being in control. But I am relieving you of your longstanding "creative" duty, so please do not take this personally. Remember, it is me and not you. See this new role as a vacation, as I create my life more effectively without unnecessary questions or fear of taking risks. I truly want to thank you again for all your lessons in service.

With much love and gratitude,
Higher Self,
Inner Management

IS FOR JOVIAL

Branch Jo•vi•al (A): In good spirits, even when life appears to be going downhill. Able to create your own joy, peace, and happiness, regardless of how hard life has hit you.

> **Rooted Experience:** *Are you creating happiness for yourself despite setbacks?*

Every Monday morning on my commute to work on the Upper East Side of Manhattan, rush hour would typically be jam-packed with a diverse pot of people from various backgrounds, cultures, social statuses, and/or career levels. Everyone seemed to share one thing in common—we were all in haste to get to some destination at the height of the morning. The sardine-tight trains made the journey even more uncomfortable. It appeared to be one of the reasons for the common disgruntled-looking faces I'd usually seen—because I was one of them.

I disliked traveling to work during rush hour, but there are times when the commute is all worth the adventure. The different entertainment options being offered by the changing faces of the many panhandlers made my trip more enjoyable and less stressful. Every panhandler had an intriguing story to tell, and I was all ears to every single one of them. Some told a story with their beautiful voices by singing their hearts out. Some told a story by break-dancing up and down the middle of the train car—if space or other commuters allowed. Others told a story by openly sharing their loss, grief, and sorrow from their own life's struggles, in most cases from substance abuse or homelessness.

"Good morning! Good morning! Good morning everyone!" One of the regular panhandlers shouted. He practically woke up everyone who was either reading the *AM New York* paper, sending messages on their phone, or catching up on sleep.

Out of all the stories to be heard, this panhandler who happened to be homeless had brought so much happiness on all the trips when I'd seen him. He was always friendly with the commuters, because that is how he made his living.

"How is everyone doing this morning? Well, I know I am doing very well today because God gave me life." He smiled at a lady who pulled her purse closer to her breast.

"Well, I am here to tell you. It's not the end of me nor is it for you. I got life. I got love. I got you to give me food. Thank you, Jesus." Some commuters burst out laughing, while others rolled their eyes at his bluntness.

Travelling from train car to train car doing magic tricks, he usually shared stories of his own life's journey—not as a victim of circumstances; more as a happy-go-lucky survivor of life's obstacles.

"Let me tell you something. I have been walking these trains for years and never saw anyone smile, even if they brushed their teeth. Did you?" He asked the young man with the earphones planted in his ears. I laughed so hard that I forgot the well-dressed man was sitting next to me.

For many years, I had seen Mr. Jove, as I called him, traveling the train by offering different entertainment to earn money. Aside from selling candies at one point, one of his most formidable accomplishments was providing comedy acts to the passengers. I would stare at him and wonder how he managed to remain so happy, even after enduring years of a rough life on the streets.

The more I observed him, the more I noticed he did not seem to care about what anyone else thought about him. With his worn-out baggy jeans, stained Lakers jersey, and black plastic bags filled with props for his acts, he kept shining his light of jokes right past some blank stares, rolling eyes, and unapproving faces. He used comedy as an outlet to create his own happiness.

"I'd really appreciate any donations you can offer. I take food and money. And if not, have a wonderful day. Remember to keep smiling. It could be worse." He bowed and held out his hat for collections. A round of claps from a few hands and a glow of bright smiles from a few friendly faces seemed to have brightened up his mood for the next train-car stage. *Damn, it could be worse.* His signature words stuck in my mind like glue all day.

As I observed Mr. Jove, perhaps there were days when he cried or days when he was angry at life. Who doesn't have those moments? Yet there was natural genuineness, sincerity, and humbleness emanating from his comedy acts of broken dreams, disappointments, and struggles. His unchanging display of joviality taught me that my own created misery from feeling claustrophobic in a tight train space was the least of my worries. His jovial nature demonstrated that it is not impossible to remain happy despite what life throws our way. If only we possessed more of his reserved nature as we rush through our days.

Trunk Insight: *Tap into Your Jovial Nature to Brighten Those Obstacles*

Do you feel that sweet joyous burst of vibrant energy flowing from your heart and soul? That radiant energy of joy feels wonderful and exciting and can brighten up the darkness in your world. Yet how can we grasp that inner light when most times we are caught up in the external miseries of challenges and suffering? We must not allow what is happening outside of ourselves to dim the beautiful, powerful life force streaming within us.

One of the main factors affecting our path to true happiness is our relationship with our environment and the people around us. At times, we depend on someone or something else to bring joy into our lives when what we seek already dwells within our soul. To attain inner peace and harmony, we must travel our own path and create our own journey to reconnect with our soulful essence. We must choose to nurture and care for our own inner peace and growth in order to traverse the obstacles in our way.

The light of our soul beams love and humbleness past any dark episode of life. You must allow your light to flow naturally into your experiences by seeing your circumstances as opportunities to expand into your greatness. Allow your inner joy to pave a new path of freedom and strength. Because, as you create your own happiness, there is a shine which can never darken your days unless you allow external factors to dim that pathway. To exert this all-encompassing inward joy, engage in more prayer and meditation, and try to smile for no reason at all.

Pray. Pray for inner balance to navigate life more gracefully. Pray for the people who have wronged or mistreated you. Pray for insight and compassion toward others and yourself; it strengthens your inner joy and unconditional love. Prayer opens the doorway to invite the omnipresent love of God into your heart. Prayer changes everything when you remain patient with the process. Trust and allow God to shine the light on any dark situation.

Meditate. Peace lies in silence. Quiet your mind and allow the flow of joy to shine its way into your reality. Meditation is a dance of thoughts to clear the debris of your constantly chattering mind. Pay attention to nothing, and immerse yourself in the pure radiant energy of divine serenity. Meditate as often as you can, and imagine yourself filled with contentment as you surrender to the moment.

Smile. While every day may not feel like sunshine and rainbows, try to smile while you can. Smiling adds longevity and vitality instead of misery and helplessness. With everything going on around you, whether it's financial issues, romantic drama, or an unsatisfactory job situation, continue to smile and be thankful for God's grace.

As you feel the wondrous embrace of happiness in your life, do not keep it to yourself. Share your smile with others, because your jovial nature may empower or uplift the spirit of someone else. Your smile may become another person's treasure and a beacon of inspiration for them to see past their own dismay.

Ask yourself, *Am I feeding happiness or sadness to myself? Is it worth the effort to focus my energy on what no longer gives me peace? Am I allowing others to create and define my state of happiness?* And as you unlock your inner Ceiba, keep in mind that it is the joyous light in your heart that gives the branches its source of power to attain true inner peace and happiness. Feed your thoughts with more positive feelings of joy, not misery about what is not working well in your life.

Leaves of Healing: *Joyful Affirmations*

Choose one hour out of each day and make it your "happy hour." If a few minutes of praying makes you joyful, then pray with a heart gleaming with gratitude. If meditation makes you content and peaceful, then meditate with the image of a bright, white light from the sky beaming down onto your crown. If smiling makes you cheerful, then smile with yourself or anyone in need of your warmth. You make the difference when you expand your jovial nature into the world.

Write the below affirmation on a sheet of paper. Fold that paper three times toward yourself from top to bottom. Place the paper in an area where it easily accessible. This could be in a phone case, in a purse, or even under your pillow. Each morning read the affirmation out loud with positive intention and a bright smile. Let these words serve as a reminder that you are a divine being of light when darkness of stress and fears try to conquer your life.

No one owns my happiness but me.

I openly allow joy to dance into my life.

I embrace the power of peace and love.

I thank God for the light shining out from my soul.

IS FOR KIND

Branch Kind (A): Warm-hearted. Compassionate. Ready to give and receive unconditional love without expectations from anyone. Considerate of oneself and others in every circumstance.

> **Rooted Experience:** *Can you be kind despite another person's behavior toward you?*

When I moved out of my shared apartment complex, it was not an easy decision to make. My love life was on the verge of a major transformation, and all possible roads to reconciliation between my boyfriend and me were fading away.

There were constant rambling thoughts—*This is my place. I was here first. Why should I leave?*—playing repeatedly through my mind. Yet, to navigate through an unexpected breakup, I had to consider the hearts at stake, the intermingling finances, and the uncertainties in the future, for my own personal benefit. All were overwhelming factors to process mentally and emotionally as I navigated a new beginning out in the world alone. After four years of investing my time and effort with someone, who would have thought that it would lead to that point?

I had watched enough Spanish and real-life novelas to grasp a fair understanding of the ins and outs of the dramatic breakup process. The sour battles over who was right or wrong. The annoying bickering about who was entitled to the funds in the joint bank account. The indecision about who owned the lease to the apartment.

Breakups can become so toxic, especially when ego and emotions are out of control.

To ensure that our split remained as amicable as possible, cooperation and compromise were necessary tactics to leverage this all-too-emotional experience. But the choice to be kind could never be that easy, as other people got involved in the situation.

"I'm so sorry, girl. I heard what happened." Kimone, a trusted coworker and friend, was calling to pay her respects. One would think someone had passed away.

"Why are you sorry? I'm good. Thanks for calling though." I sat in my temporary bedroom space at my father's house, where I sorted out the credit card bills we shared and prepared for my new life chapter as a single lady.

"Wow, you're too good. Way too good, I think." She stated.

"What do you mean by that?" I became instantly annoyed by her comment.

"I mean. Yuh too nice! Fuck him! Any other Jamaican woman would have kicked his ass out or burned his clothes if he cheated on them. I would never leave my place to no man!" She sounded angry.

"Well, it's for the best. Even though we had our problems, I have to be calm here." My defense was on high alert, but I took a deep breath to regain control of my emotions.

"Ok, but if it was me—" she continued on the other end of the line. Suddenly, I remembered all the other persons who said "if it was me" too many times.

Although there were floods of opinions rolling through my thoughts, there had been no changes in how I planned to handle the situation. "She's so weak and naive." Whispers of relatives and friends lurked through texts and were forwarded to me by others. "She has no luck with men." whispers trickled down through the grapevines. The gossip weighed heavily on my neck and shoulders with stress and embarrassment. Yet, regardless of what anyone thought about my decisions, I had to trust my instincts, and I moved strategically with patience and kindness.

Kicking him out on the street would not resolve any of our differences.

"Well, that's how you feel, Kimone. I do things differently." I'd just about had it with her comments, but I understood why she felt that way.

Not so long before, Kimone went through a horrible divorce from her husband of three years. They fought and bickered about everything, only to separate in bitterness and resentment over their finances and the kids. Her advice on how to settle my issues with my ex-boyfriend fit with the stereotypical model of an angry, bitchy black woman. That act was far from my true nature. However, the more I tuned in to Kimone's comments, the more I recognized how irritated she became by simply talking about love and relationships in general.

Her own frustrations opened my eyes to how much time, power, and energy emotional breakups can truly vacuum out of a person. I felt sad about the entire situation, but the drama was not what I wanted. For my own inner peace, being kind was the wisest strategy to dissolve the external turmoil.

My main intention was to show compassion and understanding towards every party involved so that we could move forward in a positive direction and rebuild our own lives. Using this approach may not have settled well with others, but it allowed me to secure a natural investment in myself. As I did this, I achieved a greater sense of inner peace and happiness, turning the next page to start a new beginning in my life.

Trunk Insight: *Be the Kind You Wish from Others*

Do you recall the story about the two women in the Yucatan Peninsula on the branch of Beautiful? As the tale continues, both

Xkeban and Utz-colel were now living in the underworld of the gods, called Xibalba. After her death, Utz-colel did not find any inner peace. She held a deep desire for the same sweet and natural scent that was flowing from Xkeban's grave. In Utz-colel's understanding, Xkeban's kindness was derived from sleeping with men and taking their souls away. She believed that if she gave her body to them, she would be rewarded by the gods with pure kindness like Xkeban.

Given another chance by the underworld gods to return to Mother Earth, Utz-colel returned as Xtabay, a witch sitting at the base of the Ceiba tree. She lured drunk or lost men who passed in her direction. Her heart was still spirited with bitterness from her previous life. She took "kill them with kindness" to a whole other level by trapping the men in her resentful vines. Over time, she remained miserable and angry at the roots of the Ceiba, creating her own definition of kindness through hatred.

Being kind is not a forced behavior but a natural flow of empathy and compassion from our heart and soul toward others, most importantly ourselves. Acts of kindness propel us in the direction of truth and wisdom. Before you react to others from a place of hurt and bitterness, remember who you are and what you are creating for the future.

Every act of kindness is a divine investment which only appreciates over time. A kind nature does not seek out approval or expect a favorable return. A kind nature emulates the light of God without judgment. Having said that, there will be moments when your kindness will be tested and pushed to the limits. Yet you have control of the situation by taking charge of how you react.

There will always be that one scenario where you feel taken advantage of or manipulated. But you always have a choice in your reaction towards it. Regardless of how someone behaves, you must use the power of discernment to respond with wisdom and grace. In every action, there is a reaction, which may manifest into something worse than what you may be prepared for. Think wisely before you unconsciously give your power and energy to any drama unfolding in your life.

If you feel angered or hurt, take a moment to feel how this behavior will serve you in the long term. Allow yourself to stop and think consciously about the situation. Feel the energy of the moment. React wisely, with an inner knowing that all is well with the Universe. There are no risks involved when you place your ego and pride to the side in order to make a positive step for your own betterment and peace. And as you display kindness, aim to set healthy boundaries in the situation. As it is stated in Peter 1:5, "Show hospitality to another without grumbling." Can it be that easy? Certainly, but only if you choose to.

You are the creator of your experiences; do not forget that. God graced you with the gift of kindness to incorporate into the most testing and challenging experiences. Use emotional wisdom as a tactic, and understand that the moment you shift your attitude is the moment you set the tone for the outcome to unfold in a positive direction. You only treat yourself with love when you remain calm with yourself and others. And, as Jesus spoke in the Sermon on the Mount in Matthew 7:12, "Do unto others as you would have them do unto you."

Now ask yourself, *Is an unneeded determination of who is wrong or right worth my inner investment?* Because no matter what you do or who you are, there will be some unexpected blows coming your way. Yet, you can control your emotions in those unsettling encounters. Stay anchored in your inner strength and knowing, and never sacrifice your integrity and peace because of another person's actions. Become a kind investment to yourself, no matter the circumstances.

Leaves of Healing: *Some Kind of Affirmations*

Find a small glass jar with a lid and a sheet of paper—enough to write three lines. During bedtime (starting on any day of your choice), write down the affirmation below on the paper. As you write, think of the paper as money you are depositing into your "kindness piggy bank." Fold the paper and place it in the glass jar. Shake the jar and place it by your bedside. When you awake in the morning, open the jar and shake it again to stir the abundance of kindness that has grown into love and compassion overnight. Let this exercise serve as a reminder that your kind nature is an investment in your own personal wealth and expansion to attain inner peace, happiness, and joy.

I am kind to myself. I give and receive love and affection.

I am kind to myself. I feel appreciated.

I am kind to myself. I always make me a worthy investment.

IS FOR LOVE

Branch Love (V) + (A): Undefinable. Unconditional. Unlimited. Universal.

Rooted Experience: *Have you found your true love?*

Several weeks had gone by since my boyfriend of two years and I went our separate ways. Willing to give this love thing one more try, I was ready to put myself back on the NYC singles market. I could not deny my heart's burning desire to keep searching for The One.

My many failed and tumultuous explorations of romance dimmed all my hopes of finding a true partnership. Although fears arose about potential suitors, I remained optimistic to experience whoever came and sparked a soulful connection. And so there I was on another dating escapade in search for the ultimate love activation.

On a beautiful spring evening in May, I perused through the dating profiles of the numerous matches on match.com. The pickup lines overflowing in my inbox, the thumbs-ups and wink-winks were all amusing, but the connections barely held my interest. After a few weeks on the dating scene, the process had become futile and bland—at least, that was the feeling as my patience began to run out. But then a mysterious stranger liked my profile picture and ignited in me an unusual urge to follow him.

Returning the like with no expectations, an immediate connection and conversation was initiated with Mr. Too-Hot-To-Handle. He appeared shy but opened up without hesitation as we talked about everything we could think of. We discussed the dramas with our ex-lovers as well as our own wishes and goals for the future. Our daily conversations entailed interesting explorations of the stars and the planets and their magical alignment with every single human. We were infused in the mix of each other with an incomprehensible attraction.

A pull so intense—we had to meet sooner or never.

Standing against my car in my bright green flowery dress on a beautiful sunny evening, I waited patiently to meet the man I had been texting and conversing with. Checking the time, I turned to face my car's window to admire the way my dress accentuated every part of my body. *Girl! you look hot,* the mirror version of myself thought back in confidence.

Beep! Beep! A car horn transported my thoughts back into reality.

Stepping out of his car, my date of the night parked behind me. He was wearing a fashionable blue shirt and well-slicked black pants, and the most beautiful glowing blue eyes I'd ever seen gazed back at me in awe. And as I smiled, he smiled as well. My heart melted like Godiva dark chocolate.

"Hi, it's a pleasure to meet you, finally. You are gorgeous." He extended his arm with a smile so bright. For a second, I thought I saw my dress shimmering on his teeth.

"Yes, you too." I stuttered. *You too? Who says that?* I laughed at myself. All my words became entangled and seemed to have disappeared. The heat rose higher from the intensity of our physical interaction. And as we walked toward our restaurant of the night, I only felt my love life turning into a grand adventure.

Under the glistening moon, he held me close in his comforting arms and kissed my forehead with his gentle lips. I felt an unexplainable magnetism toward him like nothing I'd ever experienced with another man. We stood in front of an immaculate church—where the silhouette of Mother Mary bowed in grace—as our hearts and lips united. With a kiss so tender, a feeling of pure magic surrounded me. *Who are you? What in God's good name is happening here?*

As I lost myself into his bright eyes, a part of my soul recognized him. Yet I was unsure of where, when, and how. And each moment our eyes interlocked, the swirling energy in my heart pulsated to another level of divine love. My heart felt the taste of heaven. My mind stepped aside to allow the moment. My soul had no objections. They all knew he was The One I wanted to spend my life with—it was a match made by Universal intervention.

Minutes, days, and weeks went by, and that instant amazing connection lingered between us. Nothing mattered anymore, as we were lost in translation in each other's arms and souls. *Whoa! I can't believe what's happening. Is this for real?* I thought, elated by the intensity of our chemistry. I held very few questions of whether this was a figment of my imagination. As we got closer and closer, all the past heartaches seemed to have erased. And, as my past failed relationships left my thoughts slowly but surely, so did he vanish along with them.

Wait a damn second. What the hell happened? No returned phone calls. No trace of him anywhere. Like a magic show, he disappeared into thin air. Sad. Confused. Heartbroken. I had no idea what happened. I did not understand why it hurt so much, and I became disappointed. *Did I fool myself here?* I thought. *I am done with love.* Love became nothing but a fantastical illusion. It was a naive and silly notion to believe that such an experience existed.

After weeks of analyzing, evaluating, reviewing, and processing what seemed to have been, I came to the conclusion that I was in an *Alice in Wonderland* fantasy. *Did I become too vulnerable?* I questioned myself. *But isn't that what searching for love meant?* Suddenly, an epiphany opened my mind to a different understanding.

I held a misconstrued perception about this entire love connection. For as long as I could remember, I had prayed for true love, but how could that be? How could I search for something that was never missing in the first place? Asking those questions and then acknowledging that truth was a hard pill to swallow but a necessary wisdom to grasp. I was thankful for that short-lived romance, which redirected me back to my long-lasting true love. I received the undeniable and unconditional love no one can ever truly give but only for me to embrace wholeheartedly from within.

Trunk Insight: *Return to Your True Love*

Love is the root of all existence. It is the unconditional, transcendental, and ever-glowing presence that weaves all things together. It is the key to returning to the true divine essence of who you are. It is your balancing and healing power aligning you onto the path of heightened awareness. Love is the nurturing care of your beautiful being past the illusions of heartbreaks and rejections. Love is your true essence. Do you believe this? Are you willing to love your true self without conditions or boundaries?

To love undeniably means to embrace the love of God from within our heart to ourselves and to every being. Yet love is a gift we must give ourselves before we extend it to anyone else. Love who you are without shame or regrets. The existing love within you holds no barrier or borders. And when you return to this divine source, an inner balance ensues and reconnects you to the radiant energy source of God.

The love of God accentuates profound bliss and carries no attachment or expectations. It's a divine love that gives and receives freely with an open heart, mind, and spirit. As you embrace the power of love from your soul, your experiences can only follow through in acceptance and contentment. Until you grasp this universal energy flowing within, there is no need to search outside yourself to give you that truth. Love will find you.

Everyone has a desire to be loved and feel affection from others. Whatever the reasons may be, only in loving ourselves can we satisfy the yearning for the completion and wholeness we seek. But what does it mean to truly love yourself? What does it take to return to the love within? What it takes is the wisdom and understanding that you are love itself, and that is your source to recognizing your power and strength to also become your greatest self.

True love is not heartache or disappointment like what we have known from our rooted experiences with others but is an inner light and sweetness that lies within the depths of our souls. As much as we adore or want someone else to love us, self-love is key to realizing and actualizing your own true happiness. View love as a kind of investment you owe to yourself.

You were beautifully crafted in the all-encompassing, loving energy of God. You are the original essence of love in all its wondrous embrace. To love wholeheartedly, believe that you are the greatest love of your life, and extend that love to others without fear or judgment. Are you willing to become this vulnerable once again? And in embracing your truth, you can unlock the quintessential energy of nature already ruminating in the light of the sun and the core of Mother Earth. Listen to your soul as it is calling for you to return to the branches of your true love from within your soul.

Leaves of Healing: *Love Yourself Notes*

Take at least five minutes a day to write down three qualities you love about yourself and why. Read them daily, while you accept and embrace them wholeheartedly. Feel free to add more features to the list as they flow through your thoughts. When you realize the true love shining in your heart, you can only attract that true love you've dreamed of. Anything can happen when you love without conditions and limits.

IS FOR MAGNETIC

Branch Mag·net·ic (A): Innately able to attract with clear intent and focus using your thoughts or words.

> **Rooted Experience:** *Are you consciously attracting your life experiences?*

I had once thought that my life was a lonely place, with few to no true friends listed in my contacts. Despite some people who were usual acquaintances, there were no real girlfriends who I could hang out with or share my feelings with. *Is it me?* I once asked myself, remembering the times when I had been misjudged, back-stabbed, or raided with jealousy. I honestly did not understand why I kept attracting the same type of friendship into my life. But all that changed when one experience made me realize what I had been unconsciously creating from my thoughts.

After many years of not seeing each other, six former high school friends and I reconnected on Facebook. To start our summer off on a fun note, we planned our first girls' day cookout at Christy's beautiful, posh house in New York City.

A bit nervous yet excited, I was uncertain how to act around them. It had been decades since we last saw each other, and there were some concerns that they would perceive me as standoffish. *I'm overthinking again. Who knows? I may have fun.* A house full of women was a sure recipe for cheerfulness, laughter, and gossip.

Our Saturday afternoon kicked off with some beautiful sunshine, soft reggae music, and glasses filled with sparkling Champagne. We got settled on Christy's soft, plush sofa and reminisced about our earlier teenage years. We rekindled wonderful moments of the failed tween love affairs, the inspiring and not-so-inspiring teachers, and the music of our ages with 'N Sync and the Backstreet Boys. *God, how we changed.* I noticed the bags under our worked-out eyes.

Enjoying the playful girl-talk, it was as if we had never left high school.

Our day could not get any better; we lived life to its fullest. Trina's strawberry crêpes were delicious. Christy's vintage wine was refreshing. The sweet savor of some well-baked weed cookies from Christy's home ingredients sent some of the girls bursting into a laughing energy.

But all that fun turned to chaos after disaster struck like gusty winds.

Thirty minutes into the party, a few of the girls became ill, possibly from the mixture of alcohol and cookies.

What the hell is happening? Why are they sick? I laughed hysterically while trying to make sense out of the moving figures wobbling in front of me.

Although I had not tasted the cookies, the strong aroma fumed my mind out of balance. Panicky and confused, two of the girls, Tamia and Shanice, danced around the living room. They had no idea what to do with themselves. Before Christy and I could calm them down, we heard knocks and noticed the cops were standing at her front door.

Help me Jesus! I'm going to jail! My life is over! But an inner voice whispered, *Keep calm. They will be gone soon.* Christy opened the door and had a brief chat with the officers, who asked over twenty questions about our little party. Supposedly, the cops had received a call from a neighbor that some girls were acting "wild" in the neighborhood.

After eavesdropping on the conversation between Christy and the officers, I turned to notice that the other girls had disappeared. No plans. Some had no shoes. No idea of where they were going. The other girls had vanished, leaving Christy and me in search of them.

What in the world did I get myself into? My head ached from all the confusion. I could not believe what was meant to be a "turnt-up" weekend had transformed into a hellish nightmare of girls high on the run.

A few days later, Trina, one of the girls who had vanished from the party, reached out to me.

"Where did you go? Christy and I called everyone." I asked, concerned.

"I have no idea what happened and how I ended up in that mess. That is not who I truly am. I felt horrible." Trina stated on the other end of the line, with disappointment and regret.

"I know what you mean. I thought my life was over." I chuckled at the lucky break of not spending the night in a jail cell.

"I cannot believe I attracted that. I know how the Universe works."

"What do you mean? The Universe?" She had lost me.

Trina began to explain how "You create your own reality" works through the law of attraction. Still puzzled, I wondered if the cookie was still running its course through her system. Yet I was intrigued by the topic; it sparked my curiosity to learn more. After several hours on the phone discussing this magnetic law connected to the Universe, as well as our crazy weekend drama, I was hooked and mesmerized by the new concept.

"Whoa, all this time I believed I was just unlucky with people," I laughed, reflecting on some past romantic encounters and a few short-lived friendships I had attracted. I had never realized that I was the creator of all those experiences and could change my storyline if I wanted.

My eyes opened to a whole new world of possibilities and potentials.

The more I tuned into my own thoughts, words, and actions,

the more I observed who entered and exited my life to adjust what experiences I had been creating on a conscious level. And in the process of acquiring all that incoming knowledge and wisdom, I was proud that God had granted me what I had asked for. I attracted a true soulful friendship with Trina, my kindred sister.

> **Trunk Insight:** *The Power of your ABCs*
> *Lies in Your Magnetic Nature*

Do you recall the many scenarios when you've asked yourself, "How did this happen to me?" or "How in heaven's name did I end up in this mess?" Not easy to understand how some people or events unfold into your life, right? And at the same time, you may have wondered whether something or someone was working magic or keeping you back in life. Contrary to what you may think, there are no coincidences or random events causing disruptions, but rather they are the results of your own thoughts, words, or actions manifesting into your reality.

You are a magnetic being who is constantly creating and innately attracting experiences, even if you don't realize it. It is important to recognize and understand your own power to create, and believe that you can consciously attract a different story. The branch of Magnetic is the divine force behind using the power of ABCs to unlock your own inner Ceiba.

Acknowledging what we've created is not an easy load to bear, especially where people are concerned or if we believe life keeps throwing negative experiences our way. Whether it was an embarrassing or a spectacular encounter, we must take responsibility for our own actions, even if we believe we are not at fault. Life is not random. Humans were not birthed from mere luck or chance. The more you realize your own innate magnetic ability, the more you realize your own power to create something different. Be open to the understanding of why certain events played out in your life and how they may assist in your own personal expansion and growth.

Facing our own creations takes tremendous courage and honesty. However difficult and outrageous an event may have manifested, your true self is always pushing you to home in to the truth of who you are: a powerful creator of your own reality. Acknowledge and accept what happened in order to address any issues and move forward. If you do not like what you are creating, restructure your belief system by shifting your focus to what you do want.

Believing is the stepping stone in manifesting what you want. Believing is the gatekeeper of the unseen path. Believing is trusting that the Universe is working in your favor, regardless of whether you see progress or movement. If you believe you are lucky, then you will most likely attract by default. If you believe you are magnetic, then you will most likely create and attract what you focus your attention toward.

Believing is the law of resonance and the power of faith intertwined. You must believe in your divine abilities to weave a new desired reality for yourself. You must believe you have that job you have been eyeing. You must believe you have that loving relationship you have been wanting. You must believe in your own talents and dreams and understand that you are exactly where you need to be.

As you experience life, know that everything is happening as it should. The path you drive now is steering you in the direction of what you want. Allow the process to flow naturally, taking little control of the outcome. When it's time to reap the benefits of your efforts, miracles or magic become second-nature because you knew your blessings were already on their way. Believe in the power of yourself to stop creating by default and start creating with conscious, focused thoughts and words.

Creating is the essence of our progression and part of the true nature of our existence. With one thought, one word, or one feeling held in focus, a seed is planted in your unconscious. Harness your magnetic ability by visualizing, imagining, conceptualizing, or fantasizing about what you want and where you are going. As the seed grows, you attract the co-pollinators, the people who are already in or who will enter your life to assist in the manifestation process.

Like a Ceiba flower buzzed with an army of bees to assist in its reproduction, your thoughts and words attract the people contributing to your expansion. Every single person is uniquely connected to the co-creation of your incoming abundance. But only you can pave the path of a new reality, because no one holds the key to your journey but yourself. No one can emotionally bind or prevent your blessings from flowing in. Within you lies the divine power to change the direction of any event. Acknowledge your own power to attract, believe that it is already done, and start creating a new life story for yourself.

Leaves of Healing: *ABC Notes to Self*

Being magnetic is a very important and powerful branch. It acts as a bridge to allow and receive what you put focus towards. To grasp the full potential of this power, remain passionate and consistent about what you want to create, and do not give up, despite obstacles and tests.

Let's return to the first three letters of your branches and create a simple mantra to remind yourself of what you can experience. Say, feel, and believe in the power of your thoughts, words, and actions.

I acknowledge who I am as a magnetic being of power.

I believe in myself and never lose faith, regardless of setbacks.

I create what I want with clear intent and keen focus on my vision.

IS FOR NATURAL

Branch Na‧tur‧al (A): Innate. Intuitive. Free-flowing and not trying to control everything.

Rooted Experience: *Will you allow your ego to destroy you?*

"Next customer in line!" I yelled out to the happy-faced lady with the cart full of bread, milk, and eggs. A major snowstorm on its way to New York City had sent everyone into a shopping frenzy.

"Hi, how are you doing?" She smiled while placing each item with caution on the conveyor belt. I did not bother to answer her, since I was wrapped up in annoyance with every customer standing on my line.

It's been a while since I took a break. I checked the slow-moving clock chiming on the wall. *Ugh, really? It can't be four hours before the end of my shift. This is stupid. Why don't these people stay home?* But every line at each register continued to extend further and further to the back of the gigantic department store.

The customers were angry from the long wait as the managers pushed for the cashiers to move faster. I became sick in my stomach from the hectic crowd around me. The busier the store got, the more stress and anxiety rushed in. *I have to get out of here,* I panicked, knowing that it would be impossible to get away from a tight shift. To remove myself from the overwhelm, I feigned illness. Certain that my plan would work, I was less concerned about what the managers thought and more focused on escaping the ruckus.

Even though I was anxious to leave the store, I battled at the crossroads of my mind about whether to stay a few more hours or not. Once I took one more look at those registers, I figured I'd take my chances with the natural events unraveling outdoors compared with the man-made disaster developing indoors.

Freedom at last! I'm out of this bitch! My manager found someone else to cover my shift.

I was proud of myself that I managed to escape the anguish. I wobbled out of the store without looking back.

As I sat on the bus heading to East New York, I decided to pay Auntie Rose a short visit instead of heading home as intended. While I was on my way to her house, the flavorful taste of McDonald's French fries kept calling out, *Terry, Terry come to me.* With an abrupt change of plans, McDonalds became the new destination of the night.

Why am I doing all of this? I questioned my erratic change of plans, but I kept going, knowing full well that the storm was strengthening ahead in my direction.

The snowflakes fell heavily like cows from heaven. The street signs were blurred out beyond recognition. And with every city block I walked, trying to resist the elements, the visibility got lower and lower. Walking across the street toward the bright neon *M* sign, I adjusted the hood of my coat to block the harsh wind from slapping my face. As I reached the middle of the crosswalk, the flashing walk sign was fading away.

Without notice, a massive blow of something heavy—it was no snowflake—slammed into the right side of my body.

Silence fell as I felt my body being thrown from the crosswalk into the middle of the street. As I landed on my left shoulder, a wave of pain rushed through my head. Unaware and partially unconscious, everything around me stopped. No cars. No sound. No voices. The snowstorm seemed to have gone. Coming back to full focus, I heard a loud screaming noise—it was the sound of my own voice.

"Am I dead?!" I screamed out to the vague silhouette of what appeared to be a man. He jumped out of his van, panting and spinning with his hands crossed on the back of his head. When I finally opened my eyes, I saw the bright hazard lights from a huge commercial van blinking in the foggy night. As he went to the driver's seat, I cried out to him in agony, "Don't leave me! Please! Don't leave me here!"

The frightened-faced man hurried toward me in panic and lifted my almost lifeless body off the pavement. As he moved me to the sidewalk, the sound of a loud crack in my left arm had both of us looking in horror.

"Ah, it hurts!" I bawled, as he tried to calm me down. Something was broken, but not as badly as my pride was.

In a matter of minutes, witnesses charged in from all direction to assist. The wailing sounds of sirens approached the scene.

"Can you tell me what happened here, ma'am?" the cop questioned, as he rallied up statements from both the driver and me. *What? Really?!?! I just got hit by a freaking van.* But an inner voice intervened to calm and check my relentless ego. *Watch yourself Terry.*

Even in pain, I forgot the sole reason for this near-death experience—my ego.

While I was in the ambulance, on my way to the hospital, tears of happiness and sadness flowed to God in how "lucky" I was. The regrets of leaving work earlier than scheduled started to seep in. I would not have suffered from a fractured arm, a painful headache, and a twisted right leg to begin with if I'd remained humble and loosened my controls of my own selfish impulses. Nonetheless, the damage was already done to my ego which almost sent me to an early grave.

Trunk Insight: *Naturally Go with the Flow, Not Your Ego*

Towering over the rain forest, the Ceiba erects its horizontal branches outwards. As the gusty winds hit the highest point, the tree remains firm in the ground due to the powerful grip of its buttressed roots. Swaying back and forth, it dances with the storm like a flamenco performer, free-flowing but holding its balance in its elongated branches and sturdy roots.

Imagine a situation appears in your life and you try to remain grounded like a tree and allow the event to take its course without effort. Is it that easy? Absolutely not. Yet, it is not impossible, especially when we allow ourselves to let go of control and flow with the experience. Unfortunately, our human self does not like that idea and loves overseeing the natural movement of things. Control can be good but can become disastrous when we allow our ego self to steer our journey ahead. With the ego in charge, we tend to discount our intuition. Before you make rash decisions, take a step back and evaluate whether a course of action will add to your highest benefit. Yet how do we know we are flowing with our intuition and not our ego?

Force and control are part of our ego nature. Through forced outcomes or impulsive actions, our ego can place us on paths we may be unprepared to face. If you feel yourself going against the wind in struggle, most likely your ego is directing your stagnation. If you feel overwhelmed and confused, most likely it is driving you into unnecessary drama. Your intuition always flows with the tides. Follow its course always, because there is no confusion—there are no questions—surrounding what feels right. And if we continue to follow the path that our ego creates for us, it may push us towards our own demise on a mental, emotional, and/or physical level.

There are ways to adapt to a current situation by simply allowing yourself to flow with the events in your environment. If it is difficult to do this, adjust your mind to a state of gratitude. Gratitude reminds us of the importance of what we already have. Make do with what is happening now until you can change the situation with a clear mind. Every day is another opportunity to appreciate the life given to you. Choose gratitude and release complaints about what you feel is not currently working well for you. When you arrive at the understanding that all experiences are temporary and subject to change, then you simply keep going, no matter the adversities or setbacks in your way. And, like the Ceiba, dancing through the storm, put your ego on pause and naturally go with the flow of your intuition.

Leaves of Healing: *I AM a Natural Invocation*

Over the years, we have allowed our egos to live wildly, directing the majority of our experiences. Yes, the ego is a natural part of ourselves, and we should not disregard its service. However, it is unnatural when we allow it to create and delve in selfish and prideful actions. We have the control and power to change things if we choose. It is time to retire our ego's services until we need to use it. And if ever you feel overpowered by your ego mind, recite the below invocation with love to remind it of who is really in control. As you say the words, feel them flowing from your heart into your mind with surety and confidence.

I AM a natural-born leader of my experiences.

I release all unhealthy contracts I signed with my ego self.

I AM a natural warrior with strength and vigor.

I flow with life's blows without regrets of my shortcomings.

I AM a natural believer that I can exert the best version of myself.

I allow my true nature to assume control of the path I'm traveling on.

IS FOR OPEN

Branch Open (V): Allow yourself to experience life if you feel it will benefit you in the short and long run. Embrace the unknown with trust.

> **Rooted Experiences:** *Are you open to trying things you once thought you would not do?*

For a long time, I told myself that, "I will never..." venture certain paths or do certain activities in my life. Here are a few examples:

- "I will never forgive any of those fucking rapists for what they did to me. I wish they would all burn in hell." In bitterness and rage, I prayed for justice. Lying in the bathtub, I cried my heart out after all the childhood traumas resurfaced in church.

- "I will never love again. Love is stupid and hurtful. I do not want it," I reaffirmed a million times over to myself. To relive another painful heartbreak and betrayal with another lover was too much to handle. I would rather be single.

- "I will never leave my job of eight years," I told myself. The amazing perks. The great schedule. The best health benefits. Everything was conveniently secured for me there. It would be a bad idea to move elsewhere. *Why would anyone risk leaving an already established position?* I thought. I may never find better than where I was.

- "I will never write another a paper in my life, I am done with all of this writing." After one whole year of trying to put my thoughts together to finish a fifteen-page graduate thesis, I was overwhelmed and drained. *Why does anyone even bother?*

Looking back at all those, "I will never…," I realize they happened all the same. One way or another, I had to experience the thoughts I had closed myself off from over the years.

- "I love you. Please forgive me. I am sorry. I thank you." Every morning before sunrise for over six months, I meditated to reconcile the hatred I held toward my abusers using the Ho'oponopono mantra. Settling our differences and moving on with my life was the best decision for my own inner peace and happiness. I never thought I would release the regret and shame of the emotional and physical turmoil from the past.

- "I am in love with you." I smiled in confidence and admiration at the beautiful, soulful eyes staring back at me through the mirror. I never knew what love felt like until I reconnected with my true self. It was a love like none other as God became the center of my heart.

- "Wow, I can't believe they offered me a job. This is surreal." Excited and ready, I gasped at the unbelievable opportunity to embark on a new career working in the mathematics field while doing finance. After taking a leap of faith to put myself out there, my dream job danced into my life without much effort. The Universe aligned what I had thought was impossible by pushing me out of my comfort zone.

- "Goodness gracious, I'm writing a book. Well, if it is God's will, then so be it." My first book project was underway despite my own fears about writing my life story. Yet the idea unlocked a new wave of confidence to inspire, teach, and motivate others as I had always dreamed of. With God as my guidance, I worried less about the details and more about when the book series would impact the lives of millions.

Trunk Insight: *Never Say Never; Be Open to the Unknown*

Do you believe in your abilities to attract your experiences through your thoughts and words? Do you believe that your life is unfolding beyond your control? Do you wonder why you are experiencing the same patterns or things you never wanted? Think for a moment about what you believe or have thought or have said, and how those beliefs, thoughts, and words have affected your reality at this present moment. If you focus on what you do not want, be open to face what might be coming on your path.

What our mind perceives, we can only experience more of. It is important to be clear and open about the mental signals we are sending out to the Universe. Be ready for what may appear on the unknown horizon ahead and release your desire to understand everything. Use your intuition to separate what serves and does not serve your highest good. Choose your thoughts and words wisely to allow an experience and ensure that it is for your own benefit, not your detriment.

At one point, you may reject the idea of trying something new and out of your comfort zone. Yet be open to the possibilities, because not everything is set in stone. For example, you may have denounced the idea of riding a roller-coaster due to a fear of heights, but there you were, screaming your lungs away in excitement. You may have refused to reconcile with a best friend because they had betrayed you in the past, but there you were, rekindling your friendship because your unconditional love surpasses the obstacles you faced together.

In those moments, the "I would never..." beliefs you once fed to yourself become "I cannot believe I just did that..." experiences. Open your mind and heart, because you may surprise even yourself. You never know what you may be missing, so be open to the unknown and allow the Universe to guide you.

Life carries no instruction manual on what to do or where to go next. No path is chiseled with arrows indicating the right or wrong steps. We never know what may unfold tomorrow. One minute we could be flying high on top of the world in success; the next minute we might be crawling low in the valley of hopelessness. Every experience is a trial-and-error phase as we aim to find happiness and peace. Be open and live.

Beyond our visible eyes, the unknown is always an inch away from affecting some aspect of our lives. How do we prepare for the unexpected? We do not. Go with the flow and open yourself to whatever life has to offer. Nonetheless, use your discernment and wisdom as you make decisions. Try as much as you can to flow with whatever comes your way. Opportunities and obstacles from the unknown will wash over our lives regardless of which path we choose. But we are strong and resilient and can transcend our own fears.

Are you ready to create better experiences for yourself than the ones created from the "I would never..." thoughts or words? Keep moving. Keep dreaming. Keep your focus on your passion and visions. Take conscious risks and live life in its splendor without fear of what may happen next. Refrain from holding on to expectations for the desired outcome. In the natural flow of the Universe, be open to anything, because your adventure awaits you.

Leaves of Healing: *Open Dialogue with Yourself*

Think of three positive experiences you said you would never do but did all the same. Write them down in a *Then vs. Now* format and self-reflect for a moment on how they manifested into your reality. Focus on the *Now* events. Do you realize how your words can actualize without much effort? Shift your thoughts to create with clear intent about what you do want. The Universe is always working behind the scenes in mysterious ways, so open your mind and heart to delve into the unknown. You might feel fear. You might feel unsure. Always follow your inner guidance when choosing to experience something different than what you already know. An example of a *Then vs. Now* is below:

Then: "I would never eat sushi. It is not cooked food."

Now: "I love to eat sushi at my favorite sushi place."

IS FOR PATIENT

Branch Pa·tient (A): Willing to trust that your fruits will bear in the right season. Grateful while awaiting your abundance.

Rooted Experience: *Can you wait for your dreams to bloom into fruition instead of rushing?*

Mother's Day weekend progressed faster than I could blink. Kevin (who is a close friend of the family) and I returned to his apartment complex to relax after a long drive from the 99 Cents store in Queens. We unloaded his car with stacks of merchandise for his new business endeavor.

Kevin was a determined entrepreneur with a long-held dream of someday becoming a wealthy businessman. Like other individuals hoping to escape the nine-to-five work life, he wanted control over his own money and time. Looking for different ways to expand his business ventures, he was always on the hunt for the next big hustle in the competitive jungle of New York City.

"What are you planning to buy for your mother?" I asked, while unpacking the baby powders, toothbrushes, and other essential items up for sale on the kitchen table. There was nothing short in his inventory—from perfumes to lotions to baby oils. If you named an item, he was most likely selling it in his mini-Walmart.

"Don't know yet. Maybe flowers? By the time I'm thirty I want to have over a million dollars in the bank."

Thrown off by his added comment, I was not too surprised by it. Because for as long as I'd known Kevin, he usually diverted our conversations, whether about eating mangoes or traveling to Europe, to always include the topic of "making it big" within the next two years.

At twenty-seven years old, he enjoyed selling and was good at it. But Kevin had a huge desire to succeed, which was driven by different ways to get rich quick.

"Yes, I can see it now." Dollar signs glowed in his big brown eyes.

"I will have a huge mansion as big as the White House," he affirmed with an unquestionable self-confidence.

Kevin was persistent like no other person I had ever met. He had great business ideas with promises of great returns, but when put into action, all his pursuits would fall like autumn leaves. I assumed this was typical for any start-up venture, but not in the way his plans trampled to the ground. Each time his endeavors failed, he bounced back with a whole new course of action, spinning on the same wheel of attraction, going nowhere. The more he rushed to make things happen, the more his invested efforts drifted off with the wind.

"It's not impossible, what you want. But you do have to wait and be smart about it. Bill Gates did not happen overnight, you know," I warned.

"Yes, that's true and I know this. But I must do this now. Life is too short and time is running by. And I can look back and say, wow, I did that." He counted the remaining potential profits on the dining table.

"Well, do what you must. But if you keep picking the fruits before they are ripe, a sour taste will always remain in your mouth." I rolled up the final pack of sheets ready for sale. With his back against the wall, counting his new lotion purchases of the day, he looked at me with a comforting yet dismissive smirk.

I admired Kevin's tenacity and optimistic nature but his plan to yield a great deal of money in a short period of time was beyond my understanding. Still, I found his impatience relatable. As I observed

Kevin's path to wealth through multiple failed attempts, I saw these same qualities in my own attempts at romantic love and friendships. Behind our efforts to succeed in these areas of our lives, we were too controlling of the desired outcome. We wanted everything too fast. Driven by high expectations and impulsive reactions, we often forgot that, truly, "love is patient" and happens in divine time.

> **Trunk Insight:** *Be Patient and Allow What Is Already Yours to Manifest*

A while ago you had planted a few seeds of ideas in your mind, hoping they would manifest in a specific time. You have used your willpower, stood firm in your faith, and taken the necessary action steps to make your ideas a reality, but nothing seems to happen the way you intended. Frustration starts to set in, and then you wonder why a stagnation is there. Before you try to push through or force the outcome, exert a bit more patience with yourself and the process. Your abundance will come into fruition if you hold on and allow the Universe to keep fertilizing your garden.

Whether you are planning to pursue a degree, start your own business, or create a new artistic project, patience should always be factored into your plans for success. No great work of art happens before it is ripe for the picking. The desperation to achieve a goal past the snail-pace motion of time may lead to unwanted failures if we do not allow the process to unfold of its own accord. It is understandable that there are times when we must shake the tree before the fruits are fully ripe to take what is ours. Yet sometimes that action step can lead to sour tastes of disappointments or regret. Before making any hasty decision on a plan, ask yourself, *Who is shaking my abundance tree? Is it my ego or my intuition?*

Use your intuition when making the next step forward. Do not allow your ego to force the outcome. With a press for time, our ego mind can form clusters of unnecessary questions, *When will I see progress? How will I manage to get this done? Why are my plans not working out?* This builds the momentum of frustration, which can propel us to take impulsive actions to pick the fruits before they are firm and developed. To pick an immature fruit is a quick way to harvest failure. At the same time, failures are necessary, because they also teach us what to do the next time if we grasp the lessons. Any fast path to success turns that initial inspiration into fears and worries of whether our plans will ever manifest. Before we know it, we reach a stage of "I give up!" Our ego will want fast movements, which can delay the abundance blooming in our gardens. Our intuition know it is coming, so hold out a bit longer and have patience.

Do not give up on what your eyes are not seeing in your physical reality. Release your controls and move forward without a press for outcomes, expectations, or the common conception that time is running out. The moment will present itself when you remain consistent and keep putting inspired efforts toward your plans. Water your garden with trust as you create a new reality for yourself.

Become open and ready to the idea that you do not have all the answers yet. The Universe is always tilling your bountiful garden, and impatience disrupts the flow of the beautiful beginning on its way. Harvesting immature plans before they blossom interrupts the reception of the true abundance accumulating on the horizon. And at any point in time when you feel stuck or nostalgic about your plans, ask yourself, *Am I moving too fast? Does everything need to be rushed to attain what I want? Do I believe I can achieve my goals without controlling the outcome?* Express gratitude to shift your focus to what you already have and immerse yourself in the present flow of the moment.

Instead of fueling conversations of "I do not have more time," start saying, "I already have what I need now." Force-ripening your goals stems from a lack of trust and balance. Rushed plans do not reap the long-term stable foundation you desire. Every success worth waiting for will bring fruitful rewards beyond your imagination. You have sowed the seeds and watered them with more ideas and motivation. You have taken the steps to push them forward. You know that the Universe supports your endeavors, so keep fueling your plan with inspiration and passion. Be ready to savor the flavor of abundance flourishing in your garden. What you want is coming; hold on with patience and trust. You are exactly where you need to be, so do not force what is already yours. As the Genevan philosopher and writer Jean Jacques Rousseau once said, "Patience is bitter, but its fruit is sweet."

Leaves of Healing: *In Due Time Affirmations*

Close your eyes and visualize yourself standing in a bright, sunny garden. In this garden, your incoming manifestations are bearing on the branch of a young Ceiba tree. There are blooming white flowers and small leaves. You acknowledge the ideas you had sown a while ago with a breath of satisfaction. As you walk around the tree, observe the fibers in each fruit slowly transforming into the fluff of abundance. It looks good, doesn't it? To know that those seeds you had planted are coming into fruition. However, be conscious, as you may be tempted by impulse to harvest that fruit before its season. Say the below affirmation three times to serve as a reminder that the Universe is already nurturing that fruit until it is ready for the picking. Be patient.

*In due time, I make wise decisions as I
move forward with my desires.*

*In due time, I trust the divine timing in the
manifestation of my abundance.*

In due time, I reap what I already know is mine.

IS FOR QUIET

Branch Qui·et (V): Bask in the beautiful moments of silence. Tune into the purity of stillness. Harmonize your mind, body, and soul in union with God.

Rooted Experience: *Have you tried to quiet the usual traffic jam of thoughts?*

For the longest while, I had considered leaving the hustle and bustle life of New York City to live in a more serene and peaceful environment. A place where I could naturally connect with myself. A place where life flows without rushing on the go. A place where nature speaks to my soul. My search for solitude began across the Hudson River, in the garden state of New Jersey. It was the perfect location to find inner peace and calmness. I believed that moving there would grant me the ultimate level of balance I had been searching for myself. At least, that's what I told myself for the longest while.

One bright Sunday afternoon as I relaxed in my sofa, I binge-watched the entire first season of Netflix's *Stranger Things*. A surge of excitement ran through me as I caught up on all the episodes I had missed over the weeks. With Oreo, my furry kitty companion cuddled next to me, I dug into a bowl of grapes, cherries, and Granny Smith apples.

"You know you don't eat apples." I said to Oreo, who gave me the squinting and begging eyes. I had no choice but to surrender to the cuteness overload. The moment felt blissful, as I felt at ease in my new apartment. Yet, despite feeling relaxed in my body, there was still that gnawing negativity of fears and worries bubbling up to the surface of my mind.

There was an unknown confusion about my life's purpose and path that lingered from New York City. I did not understand why, but I noticed constant feelings of loneliness and emptiness in the world. *Why did I move to Jersey? What am I running away from? Why do I still feel lost even though I changed locations?* The surge of questions arose from out of nowhere.

And, as much as I tried to watch the TV show, my mind would not compromise. Instead, it was channeling another show of emotional episodes emanating from within my thoughts.

Maybe I should start dating again? Ms. Loneliness suggested to ease the insecurities about living single in my thirties.

But that guy just left you. Admit it, you will be lonely with the cat forever. Ms. Judgmental perpetuated the stereotype that someone who lives alone with a pet is lonely and miserable.

No, that's not true, Ms. Confidence battled back. *I am exactly where I need to be. It's all part of God's plan.*

Oh no! I think I made the wrong decision moving here, Ms. Worry interjected.

Nonsense. You wanted balance and peace. You've found it right here in Nutley, Ms. Independent reassured everyone.

Back and forth. Back and forth. I went on and on with myself in confusion. The spiral of emotions created a traffic jam of thoughts backing up from every direction. The past heartbreaks. The present loneliness. The future uncertainties. All piled at the intersection of my mind, beeping for attention.

I dreaded the worst of a mental breakdown while my negative thoughts suffocated me to the living room carpet. Something felt amiss, and I was unsure what to do about it. There was a mysterious emptiness as the inner chattering continued to pull me deeper into a cenote of darkness. As I panted heavily, a rush of electricity and chills trickled through my body. To ease my labored breathing, I called out to the only source of peace I believed in.

Dear God! Please help me! Am I going nuts in Nutley?! I don't know what to do anymore with myself! I don't understand anything in this life! I had never felt more lost and emptier.

There were feelings of resentment I held against others and feelings of abandonment I had endured in my childhood. Every pain, turmoil, and piece of baggage I held onto overflowed like a raging river in tears. My emotions were feeding the pain and hurt which I thought I had rid myself of. However, as the thoughts and emotions kept going, a wisp of silence overtook the negativities.

Submerged in a meditative state, I drifted off into a dark stillness. No words. No sounds. No movements. My mind and my heart streamed in sync as I lay in the quiet flow of nothingness. After several moments, a wave of profound inner peace and wisdom engulfed me. *What in heaven's name just happened?* I asked myself. I tried to comprehend the unbelievable spiritual occurrence.

Something was different around me, aside from Oreo's bright green eyes staring in my face. My eye and soul opened to a new light of understanding that all would be well with God in my life.

During that meditation, there was an unexplainable oneness with God and everything around me. It showed me that I had the wrong idea about finding peace for myself. The peace I had sought could never be grasped outwardly, but was an inside job I had to experience. The more I quieted my thoughts to tune into God's love and power, the more peace flowed into my external environment.

Trunk Insight: *Quiet Your Mind as Much as You Can*

Is it ever easy to quiet our minds when there are at least twenty things constantly streaming through our thoughts? The unfulfilled path and dreams that are unseen on the horizon. The events that are interplaying in the present moment. The past experiences that have taught us lessons. On top of that, there is the bombardment of information fueling into our brains daily. From social media to work to even our own home environment, it can feel difficult and overwhelming to maintain a state of inner peace and balance. At times, we may feel like running away from it all, leaving family, friends, and other people behind. Yet it is important to understand that no matter where we go or who we are around, true peace can be unlocked when we aim to quiet the usual mental traffic jam, and reconnect with God in ourselves.

Our thoughts will never stop, even when we attempt to block them. They will come. But we have control of what we feed to ourselves. Allow the thoughts to rise, and observe them with understanding and kindness. However, do not give the negative thoughts the power to control your emotional state of wellness.

What our mind cannot grasp, our soul understands fully. Whatever answers we seek about ourselves dwell in the depth of our inner existence. You have the key to unlock your inner power by connecting with the divine essence of yourself. There is a profound peace and clarity when you make the time to reconnect with God, beyond the noise of everyday living. To do this, we must seek the exit in our own built-up mental prison. Quieting our mind is a gateway past the interference of our external environment. We achieve a state of inner flow and oneness when we engage more with our soul by incorporating the power of prayer and meditation in our daily rituals.

Through meditation or prayer, we pave the way for our soul to wholeheartedly guide us past our own fears and worries about life. You must allow yourself to drift into a void of nothingness away from feelings of unnecessary suffering and discontentment. Silence is the holder of the truth you seek. Silence is the flame of inner wisdom and peace. Silence opens the doors to the spiritual essence of self. Your soul knows the answers; give your mind rest and let go of control by relaxing in quietness.

Life can become a balancing act of movement, relaxation, and living in the moment. To balance our ever-rampant thoughts, sometimes we must aim to do nothing and be quiet for thirty seconds or even an hour. In being quiet, you allow yourself to find the peace you have longed for. In being quiet, you create harmony in your mind, body, and soul in oneness with God. In being quiet, you fuel inner joy and happiness into your life. Try to clear your mental traffic jam of thoughts by meditating and praying as often as you can. Quiet your mind and allow God to lighten up those dark times in your life.

Leaves of Healing: *Do Nothing Exercise with "Ode on Solitude"*

Stop what you are doing at this very given moment. Stop reading. Wait a minute, keep reading. Stop wondering about how many chapters left to finish in this book. Breathe in a long, deep feeling of peace, love, and gratitude, then breathe out any clustered negativity connected to insecurities, worries, and pain with a gentle "ahhh" to release those extraneous thoughts. Do this exercise daily for five minutes. Feel yourself release the thoughts piling in your mind. Open your heart and allow the moment to flow into nothingness with God.

> *Blest, who can unconcern'dly find*
> *Hours, days, and years slide soft away*
> *In health of body, peace of mind,*
> *Quiet by day.*
>
> *Sound sleep by night; study and ease,*
> *Together mixed; sweet recreation;*
> *And innocence, which most does please,*
> *With meditation.*[1]

---

1 Excerpt from "Ode on Solitude," Alexander Pope, 1688–1744

IS FOR RESPECT

Branch Re•spect (V): Care for and consider yourself and others as you handle your business. Be neutral in your emotions and try to see things from a different perspective. Be the light despite misunderstandings.

> **Rooted Experience:** *Do you give the respect you wish to see from others?*

Standing in line, I waited for the check-in process to move faster at the County Hospital in Brooklyn.

"Next patient!" The receptionist shouted from the registration counter. Her colorful nail extensions signaled for the next person to approach her desk.

Oh, that's me. I walked over with my medical forms already completed to avoid engaging with her.

"Sign here and here. Sit until your number is called," she instructed, keeping her face down in the paperwork. Pointing her long fingers, she directed me toward the patient seating area, which was close to her.

I guess nothing has changed here. I rolled my eyes at the filthy seats and the way she had dismissed me. I had no idea why I was annoyed, since I was already used to the terrible customer service experience when I visited there.

Like the DMV and large retail stores, public hospitals were my least favorite places to do business. Drama and bad attitudes were likely to occur, regardless if you were nice or a smiling star. *Perhaps she is having a bad day.* I wanted to give her the benefit of the doubt. But then one of her colleagues stopped by to visit.

"Hey girl! What are you doing tonight?" Her coworker giggled.

"Hey, it's book study night and the kids are coming over," she laughed aloud with the most vibrant personality I had heard all morning.

Really? I raised my eyebrows, noticing the quick shift from her aggressive tone to a friendly demeanor. *Try not to judge,* an inner voice reminded. Minding my own business, I checked if I was the next number on the call board to see the doctor.

"Next patient!" she shouted, louder than before. I cringed at her high-pitched voice, certain that one of my eardrums had ruptured.

"What is your name?" the receptionist asked the soft-spoken, tiny-framed lady standing at her desk. This patient had angelic poise, as she calmly answered her. In a beautiful floral dress and carrying a hand-woven bag, the lady had a beaming smile that would brighten up anyone's day.

A smile I had never seen before in that place.

"Why do you need to see the doctor? Do you have an appointment?" the receptionist checked the lady's paperwork.

Unfortunately, the lady had not completed the medical forms in their entirety, as instructed, and had to suffer a barrage of questions.

"Where are you from?" the annoyed receptionist asked the lady, as she perused through the forms.

"Suriname," the lady answered with a soft voice.

"Ma'am, I did not ask for your surname. I asked where are you from? Don't you understand English?" the receptionist shouted at her. Her loudness caught everyone's attention in the waiting room while the lady stood frozen. At that point, I was unsure whether to laugh or to get upset, but an inner voice advised, *Be mindful with your reaction.*

"That's not what she meant, ma'am," I interrupted from my chair, which was just a few feet away from the counter. I glanced at the angelic lady, who seemed too timid to respond.

"She said *Suriname*. It's a country in South America. You misunderstood," I explained. With a deep breath, I expected a blowout from the receptionist. Locked and loaded with defense, I was prepared for a rude comment. *Dear Jesus, take the wheel!*

"Oh, really? I didn't know that. I'm very sorry ma'am," she apologized to the lady.

"It's okay. I understand," the angelic lady from Suriname responded in the same composed manner. "I get that all the time." She laughed it off.

Surprisingly, the receptionist's attitude became less aggressive and more engaging with us. All three of us erupted into laughter at the huge misunderstanding.

For some reason, I sensed a warmth and compassionate energy emitting from the receptionist's smile. Perhaps she expected drama as much as I did, since it was the usual encounter at the hospital. Perhaps she was used to giving or receiving little respect from others. Yet the angelic lady had managed to remain calm despite the receptionist's initial rudeness with her. If I were in the lady's shoes, I would have reacted in defense. But the lady's attitude demonstrated that it was possible to be neutral, patient, and respectful to others while taking care of business, even in an unfriendly environment.

Trunk Insight: *Be the Respect You Wish to Experience*

It does not matter where you go or who you are; bad attitudes, misjudgments, or arrogance will find their way onto your path through a person or from a collective group. When they do, remind yourself, "I am a creator. I own my attitude in every circumstance." No one can tell you how to behave, but aim to demonstrate the respectful attitude you wish to receive all the same. Only you can create a more positive feedback loop by showing that respect. What you give out, you will receive, regardless of how others behave.

Respect is caring to align in your own truth and power before reacting out of anger or impulse. Sometimes when we interact with others, we expect them to treat us a certain way to appease us. But life is not always this way, so release any expectations about how someone should act in the moment. Keep in mind, there will be cases of something or someone pushing your buttons, but you are the one in control of your experiences, not them. Regardless of wherever you may be or whatever is happening around you, try to be open, understanding, and patient for your own inner joy and peace.

Our ego may say, *Why should I be the one to apologize?* Or *Why should I be the first one to be nice?* In situations where everyone wants to be right and no one wants to be wrong, this is a distasteful scenario for ignorance and bigotry to boil over. In moments like those, reconnect with your truth. Your true self does not judge but remains neutral in negative situations by never taking anything personally. It communicates clearly by setting healthy boundaries with others in elegance and humbleness. If you struggle with annoyance or irritation because of another person's behavior or actions, try to see things from another perspective.

Not everyone understands what they can create with their own words or actions. Not everyone is willing to acknowledge how their own unkempt emotions can worsen a situation. Not everyone is you, so aim to be the light in negative experiences. What's important is that you give the respect for your own self, not to please anyone else.

Remain conscious of what you magnetize in your surroundings. Be mindful that your ego self makes assumptions while your true self shows care and consideration for others, but most importantly yourself.

Take a snapshot of the below affirmation in your phone. Ensure that it is accessible in times when respect is called for in a public environment. Whether at the clinic, bank, shopping mall, or DMV, you own the situation when you give the respect you wish to see from others.

*I **Remember** who I am in dealing with others.*

*I **Embrace** my truth with divine power.*

*I **Show** respect for my inner peace and happiness.*

*I **Practice** patience and let go of judgments.*

*I **Expect** nothing from anyone but myself.*

*I **Consider** all options before reacting on impulse.*

*I **Thank** God for guidance as I handle my business.*

IS FOR SUCCESS

Branch Suc•cess (A): Following your soul's guidance as you aim to fulfill your own wishes and dreams. Moving forward with passion and purpose despite delays, critics, or failures.

Rooted Experience: *Who decides your path toward success?*

Auntie Joy's Labor Day party was in full swing in her spacious and nicely mowed backyard. Everyone I knew was in attendance, from distant cousins to close family friends; all mingled together and raved about my aunt's delicious jerk-chicken, macaroni salad, and sweet corn on the cob.

Sitting under a large tent to shield myself from the piercing rays of the sun, I unwrapped an ear of sweet buttered corn from the aluminum foil to feed my rumbling stomach. As I got ready to sink my teeth into the heavenly flavor, Karen, a family friend who I had not seen in years, approached me with arms wide open.

"Terry! Oh my goodness! You have grown so big!" She squeezed my life force out of the chair.

"Hi, Auntie Karen."

I smiled as I was ecstatic to see her as well. Growing up in Jamaica, almost every family friend who looked older than I did was either an auntie or an uncle for the sake of respect.

"The last time I saw you, you were this high." She measured her hands to her waist.

"Wow, and now you are sixteen, right?" I must have been eight or nine years old when I had last seen her pretty face.

"Yes, I am." I sat up straight to address her like a grown-up.

"I heard you're doing very well in school. What are you planning to do after high school?"

I guess I'll finish this later. I thought of the savory corn dripping butter in my hands. Sealing the wrapper shut to keep the warmth intact, I braced myself to discuss one of the most commonly asked questions from the adults.

In my earlier childhood years, I wondered why the older folks initiated their conversations about school. The "What do you want to be when you grow up?" usually irked the hell out of me. I appreciated their consideration for my future, but I would rather have had a regular conversation. "How are you feeling today?" I wished they would ask. I was happy to share the emotional inner turmoil of an insecure teenage girl. "What do you do for fun?" I wish they knew how much I planned to travel the world once I figured out my financial plans. But school seemed to be the only available and automatic question to strike up small talk with a child.

"Well, I'm thinking about becoming an actuary, but maybe a mathematician," I replied. Her bright, bold brown eyes widened with an impressive and surprising look.

"Wow! Oh, okay. Smart girl. That's interesting and very difficult—I guess you really like a challenge." She seemed to be taken aback by my response. "And you know something? I always thought you would do great in the medical field. You can make good money and it's secure." *Here we go again!* I smiled at her.

To be honest, I was not too surprised by her suggestion, since I had become used to being offered other financial alternatives, especially in the medical field.

"Umm, actually I get squeamish at hospitals and clinics," I joked.

"Haha. I guess everyone does. But you cannot go wrong in medicine. It's a good backup option when things do not work out as planned. I learned that the hard way."

Karen had recently completed her Bachelor of Science degree in Nursing to join the growing list of medical professions already established within or close to the family. Earning that degree was a major success for her, especially after experiencing her own failure, having dreamed of one day becoming an engineer. But for me becoming a nurse was not the path my soul urged me to follow. The financial security was inviting, but I knew it was not my dream. My heart and soul chose the path of numbers, and so I fueled that life force with vision, trust, and patience in the unknown.

"Hey, baby, are you ready?" Her handsome boyfriend interrupted us before I got to reply to her comment.

"Well, my dear, it was nice seeing you. Stay beautiful, and good luck with the math thing. I really hope it works out." She hugged me and walked out of the party, leaving me confused and less hungry for the tasteless corn, now frigid in the wrapper.

Oh Lord! What if she is right? Maybe I am in over my head with this whole math thing. What if I fail like her? I must have a plan B if this doesn't work out. I panicked. Our brief conversation had me rethinking everything. I had not imagined that Karen's questions and comments would stir up so much doubt and anxiety surrounding my future. At the same time, there was a deep knowing that I was on the right path.

Regardless of the doubts, I held firm in my heart that my goal to become a mathematician would manifest someday, somehow. I was not concerned about when it would happen, how I would pay for school, or what I would be doing. My only plan was to follow my soul's guidance. And, despite the failures, criticisms, and challenges that showed up along the way, I continued toward the path of success with the purpose and faith. As I pursued what I love, the Universe conspired to make my dreams a reality.

What if I do not become successful like others? What if my life does not work out as planned? What if I am deluding myself with these crazy ideas? If your mind has asked any one of these questions at some point in the planning process, stay the course and keep moving, because you are on the right path towards what you want.

When there is a burning desire fueling in your heart, be ready for anything coming on your path. Even with motivation and passion, fears, doubts, confusion, obstacles, or criticisms will arise regardless of how well-defined your plans are. Nonetheless, you do have a choice of who or what you allow to dissuade your vision. It is important to trust and believe in your unseen creations while you continue to build on your dreams. There is one seat behind the wheel, and only you hold that special key on the road to manifesting what you want.

Success is within you. There are no limits to what you can achieve as you do the work. You must hold firm to the belief that your fruits are already there. There will always be different anomalies on the horizon to cope with. But you can create your own rules of engagement to stay the course of arising doubts and uncertainties. Here are three takeaways from the branch of Success you can utilize as reminders:

A: I define my own path to success.

What does success mean to you, and why? It is imperative to be mindful of what you define as being successful. It should not be defined by focusing on what others have already achieved in their lives or on mere material gains. Success should be aligned to your dreams and what you decide for yourself.

Chasing another person's dreams offers no fruitful benefits, nor any freedom to be yourself. Most successful people have been through many roadblocks. Can you handle the challenges and obstacles they endured? You can use their experiences as inspiration and motivation to start following your own path. Success involves becoming a leader within yourself by pursuing your own soul's knowing, not another person's accomplishment.

Whatever you want is attainable. The investment in your own path can manifest a desirable outcome if you keep focus on your vision. Material abundance may show up as an added reward but should never be the main intended focus to begin with. Focus on the purpose at large not the payments involved. As you stay focused and steer your direction forward with continued passion, you never know what gifts or rewards you can accumulate when you follow your own path.

B: I follow my inner guidance and stay open to outer guidance.

There will be persons who will share opinions on what you should do, how you should proceed, and/or why you should take a certain path in your life. Do not discount their suggestions and insights. Listen, observe, and be open to their messages, because their feedback may push you forward with strength and determination. Instead of viewing their comments as criticism, judgment, or discouragement, view them as lessons in discernment to reevaluate whom you share your dreams with. Sometimes, it is best to keep your goals to yourself until you are confident in your plan of action.

At times these individuals may share advice from a place of care and kindness, and other times it is a projection from their own negative experiences. It is your decision what you accept, because not everyone's life story is aligned to your journey. With every piece of advice you receive, take away what resonates and discard what is not for your potential benefit. When you know what you want and why, you choose a certain path. What others say holds little influence on what is already determined by your soul and driven by your heart.

C: My failures are progress toward success.

Failure is inevitable on the path to success. Failure and success work hand in hand like the branches work with the roots of a tree. When a branch has fallen to the ground and has decayed over time, it slowly merges itself into the roots of the tree as part of the growth and development process.

When obstacles strike on your journey, reevaluate, reflect, and find ways to integrate that struggle into the process. Readjust what is not working to assess a new possible direction. Learn from the failed outcome and grasp the wisdom it was trying to teach you. Use the opportunity to draft a new course of action from a different vantage point and allow any new ideas to flow from within your soul.

When it seems as if your dreams are fading away before you, do not give up. Do your best to embrace the lessons in the obstacles to overcome them. You must be open to surrender to the temporary nature of the events. If you feel trapped on a specific path, refocus your mind and intention on that initial inspiration you felt.

Why did I start, again? What was my true purpose here? That initial drive can propel you to restart that same endeavor. The burning desire for what you love to do may be dimmed by an unexpected failure. However, know that your dream is never extinguished. Refuel the fire with the trust that was already fueling from your heart and soul. Your success depends on your patience and the belief that you already have what you want. Decide whether you will allow failures to keep you stuck or push you to never give up. The journey of life comes with thorns and curves; yet you are strong enough, powerful enough, and wise enough to bend and pass through them.

Have you thought about who you allow to determine your path? Is it you or someone else? Are you ready to build your own dreams and persevere despite failures or oppositions? Can you handle the success that is coming toward you? Say the below affirmations whenever you feel undeserving or uncertain about the path you are traveling now. As you say the words, feel yourself climbing the branch of Success with passion and meaningful purpose. There are no limits when you follow your own truth.

I am success—I set clear intentions.

I am success—I follow my heart's passion.

I am success—I connect with my inner guidance.

I am success—my failures are my ascent of progression.

IS FOR TRUST

Branch Trust (V): Have faith and confidence in yourself and the unseen journey ahead. Surrender your fears and doubts to God. Believe in God's plan for your life.

Rooted Experience: *Do you trust in yourself?*

"Do you have a book within you? Start writing your own life story today!" *Really, again?* I gasped in amusement as another Facebook ad flashed across my news feed for the fifth time in one day.

Just a coincidence. It doesn't mean anything, I tried to convince myself, although I agreed with the consensus that "everything happens for a reason." Scrolling past the ads, I felt an urge to explore these "mere coincidences," but I was too caught up in my own fears and doubts to even entertain the idea of writing a book.

Writing was a major struggle for me for as long as I could remember. Listing numbers or talking on the phone were easier than putting pen to paper or sending texts. Even as a business professional, the thought of sending emails at work usually left me scrambling and reviewing the content of the messages three or four times over. To discover or believe that I had some hidden talents in authoring was nerve-wracking to say the least.

For years I accepted myself as a "bad writer" after receiving Cs in college and being told by a former high school English teacher to "stick with numbers." I arrived at the conclusion that I was good in math and terrible in English. To be good at both was an impossibility.

My soul kept highlighting these unconscious aspects of myself, but I distrusted and ignored my abilities, among other things. No one knew that I was also a natural intuitive with spiritual gifts.

Growing up in a religious environment in Jamaica, I held a keen awareness of my spiritual abilities. Prophetic dreams, visions, and the voices of angels and spirits came to me naturally at five years old, but I never told anyone for fear of ridicule and judgment.

In my culture, most individuals associated with the spiritual realm outside of the church were perceived either as evil or as conjuring the devil's work. To protect myself from being ostracized, I suppressed that part of myself and never discussed angels or spirits with anyone else, even with the people closest to my heart.

"People that do such things go to hell. The *Bible* clearly speaks against them." A cousin expressed her disgust for individuals who use their spiritual gifts to help others. Little did she know that one of those people was a close loved one sitting next to her. *I wonder how she would react if she knew about me?* I thought to myself.

"God will punish them. They are selling their souls to devil." She made it clear to me what would happen to anyone who followed that path. Confused about her reasoning, I asked God, "What should I do? It does not make any sense." My soul was calling me to inspire and motivate others using my spiritual abilities. On the other hand, fears about what others would say left me unhappy and unfulfilled. Therefore, I asked God to please take these abilities away. But I knew I was only denying my own truth.

I treated my gifts as a curse instead of accepting them as a blessing. It was frightening and frustrating to feel another person's emotion while in a public place or know what was happening in someone's situation without them saying a word. And, as much as I believed in God, guardian angels, and the power of faith, I held little trust in myself. I kept repressing the truth of who I was in order to not inspire and motivate others through my spiritual work.

However, the more I trusted in God's plan, the more divine guidance poured in from all directions in my life. New friends. New business ideas. New and improved self-empowerment. The fears I had about being ridiculed disappeared over time. My mind and heart were infused with the power of trust and patience. Slowly but surely, the unnecessary worries of what others would say or what I believed as the truth transformed into believing more in the higher power at play in my life's path and purpose.

Trunk Insight: *Trust in Yourself Regardless of What Others Might Say*

Extending across the canopy of the rainforest, the Ceiba's elongated branches shield an array of trees and house a diverse group of creatures. It shelters the giant prehistoric harpy eagle family on top of its crown. It allows boa snakes to live inside its thick bark. Yet it continues to grow and bear bountiful fruits, even during the driest seasons. In all its vulnerability, the Ceiba is trusting of the process. Regardless of how the creatures and the weather interact with it, the Ceiba knows that it is all part of the natural alignment of its expansion and development. Can you become this trustworthy or so vulnerable in yourself in order to expand beyond your comfort zones?

Trusting yourself is necessary to follow your purpose and grasp your full potential. Do not lessen your talents, despite doubts, fears, or criticisms. To trust in you is to trust in God. But sometimes it is easy to turn a blind eye to our soul calling, if we lack belief in ourselves, and place the opinions of others before our own truth.

A lack of faith is one of the many reasons preventing us from entering the new beginnings in God's plan. How can we openly accept or follow a new direction in our lives when our mental dialogue is infused with phrases such as "I don't know what others would say" or "I don't think I can do it." You never know what is for you until you step out in faith and embrace another level of yourself. Having said that, always use your intuition and discernment to move into an unknown path.

If you feel pushed onto a certain path, there is most likely an innate ability to develop or a lesson to learn. It will scare you. It will stir you. It may possibly elevate you. The only way to know is to allow and surrender to that experience. Your soul puts you on that path for a reason. There is a guiding light within, illuminating your gifts or talents or endeavors that are meant to broaden your horizons. Embrace these innate abilities rooted deeply within yourself. They are ready to be unleashed into your life when you let go of your fears.

Trust in your own inner power that you can do more than what you had thought possible. As you make the effort, surrender the need for evidence and expectations of the outcome, because what is yours will come to you. It is understandable that letting go can be difficult, especially when our ego interferes and feeds our thoughts and words with old negative patterns. When your ego wants control, instead of allowing those limited affirmations ("I cannot do this") to rule over your thoughts, address your ego by saying, "Sorry, I did not call upon you." This reminds your ego of the contractual agreement you made with it on your powerful branch of Intuitive.

Before the physicist Albert Einstein published his infamous theory of relativity, $E=MC^2$, denoting that energy and matter are the same, fear of objection was most likely a factor. Yet he published it anyway. Before President Nelson Mandela led the movement to end apartheid in South Africa, fear of oppression was most likely a factor. Yet he led the movement in strength and faith. They followed their own path and pursued what others might deem as ridiculous or belligerent. They had to trust in themselves despite the obstacles they encountered. It probably made little difference to them who accepted or acknowledge their truth.

You are no different from these great pioneers in their own

elements. Believe in what you want to accomplish for your future. Open yourself to the unimaginable by becoming vulnerable in the unexpected and unknown paths. Learn to trust in God's guidance and allow the ideas to flow from your soul.

There is a bounty of brilliant ideas lying dormant in the abyss of your subconscious mind. Tap into those inner abilities to activate them, and trust what is being manifested into your life. Suspend your analytical mind for a moment and look to the light of your higher self. Take that leap of faith forward with that plan of action, without questions or regret.

How many times has God pulled through for you? How many times has your inner strength been tested? When God is in your plans, there should be no questions or doubts but only patience, trust, and acceptance of the path. Sometimes life unravels more about us than what we want to acknowledge. Release any need to fully understand everything in the moment.

As you move forward, uncertainties and obstacles will continue to arise to test your faith. They may dampen your spirit to persist or distract you from the true vision, but never surrender your faith to the temporary nature of problems. You are unlimited, with the magnetic abilities to attract what you want in your life. Integrate more trust in your inner dialogue to manifest what is already yours in divine time.

Leaves of Healing: *A Prayer to Trust in God*

The below prayer serves as a resource for you to use when questions arise about your path or if you feel trapped by worries and doubts about yourself. Write the prayer down and keep it close to you. Prayer changes everything with pure intent and belief. Know that all is well as you release your doubts to God.

Dear God,

I come to you in this hour.

I ask for guidance to help release my fears about myself.

Please give me the strength to realize my own inner power.

Help me to trust that all is working in my favor.

Thank you,

[Your Name]

IS FOR UNLIMITED

Branch Un·lim·it·ed (A): Ready to grasp the infinite and endless possibilities that life has to offer you. Set to tap into the boundless potentials within yourself.

> **Rooted Experience:** *Are you holding yourself back from your greatest life because of fears or doubts?*

Oh my goodness! This is so embarrassing! I panicked. With my back against the stall in the women's restroom at work, I attempted to fit the thread through the needle's eye—to mend my broken pants from ripping any further down my thighs.

I was thirty minutes away from one of the most important, life-altering job interviews of my career within the company I worked for. But as much as I had prepared myself for that day, everything, including my mind, went haywire.

Not only was the last-minute suit I had purchased from Macy's falling apart, but my nerves were all over the place. My mind jumped between fears and doubts about whether I was in over my head on this once-in-a-lifetime leadership opportunity.

All patched up, I returned to the reception area with a fake smile plastered across my face— to hide the embarrassment. The inner angst climbed as I checked the clock—my interview was now less than ten minutes away.

My heart raced like greyhounds. My palms sweat like morning dew. More doubts arose to contemplate.

"She's too young."

"She doesn't have enough experience as a manager."

"She's not as open as others."

The rampant whispers I had overheard from other colleagues kept reinforcing the fear that I was undeserving and unqualified for such an important leadership position. In addition, I was reading through the job posting details to review all the prospective responsibilities—as well as the preferred education and experiences.

Oh man! No way I'm getting this job, I sighed in disappointment as I compared the posting description to my current résumé. I frowned at the irrelevant job experiences I had included to boost my credibility as a manager. The more I perused the posting, the more negative thought patterns surfaced. I even entertained the thought that my education background might not be the perfect fit for what the company wanted.

The posting had outlined, "Education: A candidate with a master's degree preferred." My bachelor's degree did not seem it would measure up to the other applicants who most likely met their preferences.

"Terry Wisdom. Hi, please come on in." One of the interviewers interrupted the negative inner dialogue and greeted me with a smile and extended arm. *Too late. It's now or never.* I followed him into the interview room.

As I entered the beautiful, spacious area overlooking the Manhattan skyline, two other committee members also greeted me with handshakes and gazing smiles. Both were top-level executives I knew and admired. Intimidation set in, as they we were also well-known and respected leaders. Knowing who they were did not lessen the negative thoughts racing on like a river. Now, there were added concerns about what to expect, what to say, and how to say it "right."

Breathe, Terry! an inner voice whispered. *You already got this!*

And, as expected, the inquisition commenced.

The questions rolled in one by one from each interviewer. I stumbled on my words a bit but took a deep breath to ease the stress of the moment. *Dear God, I hope they don't notice my ripped pants. Focus, Terry!* A nervous wreck I was.

But somehow, I felt empowered once I sat comfortably in the "hot seat." A sudden glow of confidence, from out of nowhere, dawned on me.

Certain about my potential as an effective leader, I answered each question with honesty and openness. My eyes interlocked with their eyes like a harpy eagle on the lookout for prey. Quick. Clear. Concise. The answers were flowing off my tongue. Although my voice became parched from speaking, I kept talking non-stop. *Damn! Who is this?* I could hear Alicia Keys' powerful voice blazing "Girl on Fire" in my head. Some undeniable force of nature awoke a sense of surety and courage within me, and I already knew I was hired.

After forty minutes of inquiries, I left the interview feeling as if I had just conquered climbing Mount Kilimanjaro, knocking the questions out of the cliffs. The confidence streak did not end there but only expanded. Afterwards, one of the interviewers complimented me on my exuberant communication skills which I'd never before realized in myself.

Months had passed when I received the news that I was the selected candidate. Ecstatic and thankful, an unbelievable feeling of being overwhelmed ensued in my heart from what I had accomplished. I could not believe I'd surpassed many qualified applicants, as well as my own unnecessary fears. *If I could do this, I can do anything,* I thought, as all my concerns of not having enough experience disappeared. No boundaries existed once I let go and allowed God to take control of the wheel of possibilities. No one or nothing (not even fashion fails) limited my potential other than the limits I placed on myself.

There is another legendary story told by the Maya people of the Yucatán Peninsula, the legend of the dwarf of Uxmal. The folklore depicts the journey of a young dwarf leader who conquered his own limiting beliefs to become a great king in the city of Uxmal, Mexico.

Once there was an old woman who lived as a hermit and could not bear any children. The woman was sad that she was alone and prayed daily for a child. She took an egg from the town's market to nurture and protect as her own. For years, the old woman waited patiently for the egg to produce a child, but nothing happened.

Then one morning, the egg hatched, and a little baby boy emerged. He raised his tiny hands and smiled at her. Excited by the blessings from the gods, the old woman raised the little boy as her own.

Years passed, and the little boy grew with love and compassion in the old woman's care but remained pint-sized like a three-year-old child. From that point on, he was called the Dwarf. The old women loved him unconditionally. She was certain that one day he would make a great king over the land.

"I want you to go challenge the king at the palace, my son. You are just as strong as he is," she instructed the Dwarf. Doing as he was told but fearful, he went to the palace to confront the king's rule.

In the palace, the king ridiculed his height and challenged him to a series of tests.

"Lift this heavy stone to test your strength against mine." The Dwarf became frightened and returned to the old woman.

"He is more powerful and stronger than I am. I cannot lift that stone," he said to her.

But the old woman replied, "Go back and show him your worth."

When the Dwarf returned to the palace, he lifted the stone to complete the strength test. He passed with flying colors, which left the king in anger.

The king proposed the second challenge to the Dwarf: "Build me a grand palace that is mighty and tall in one night, or you will die by tomorrow." He thought that the Dwarf would not accomplish this test because of his size. But by morning the Dwarf had built an amazing pyramid. His unbelievable accomplishment only made the king angrier.

Finally, the king assembled his court and challenged the Dwarf to a fight.

"I shall strike you with a bundle of cogoiol (a type of hardwood) and if you survive, then you can strike me back." The king was sure he would kill the Dwarf this time around. The Dwarf became very afraid and returned to old woman for guidance.

"The king wants to kill me," he said to her.

"Do not worry. All is well with you," she reassured him.

The old women placed a tortilla on the Dwarf's head and sent him back to the court, where the king gathered all his representatives to view the death of the Dwarf and display his power and strength.

When the king struck the Dwarf, the Dwarf did not break nor did he fall. He survived the massive blow to his head. The king became afraid of the unlimited power of the Dwarf's resilience and faith.

Now it was the Dwarf's turn. With one hit to the head, the king was dead. His successful completion of the tests led the Dwarf to become the king of the great city of Uxmal. After he attained rulership, the old woman disappeared and was never seen in the city again.

The legend continues that she sits at the base of a river, under a great tree with a serpent beside her. That great tree is believed to be the Ceiba, which shelters everyone with the unlimited stretches of its branches.

While there are many existing versions to this inspiring story, like the story of Xtabay, the key takeaway is to never doubt in your unlimited self. You can become so much more in life when you face your own fears and expand your potential. There are no limits to what you can accomplish or become on your journey. When you realize who you are as an infinite soul using the mind as a tool, you can overcome the fears blocking your growth, success, and expansion. Like the dwarf king of Uxmal, release any conditioned beliefs about what you can do, actualize your potential, and remain true to you.

Release your limited beliefs. What limiting beliefs are you feeding to yourself? You may have wanted a job opportunity but felt you were unqualified for the role. You may have wanted to earn your degree but felt you were not intelligent or did not have the finances to enroll in school. For far too long, your beautiful, ever-chattering mind focused its attention on what you could not do. Do you agree that it is time to retire those old beliefs off your inner résumé?

Fears will surface. They are a part of the natural process of being human. Our fears are created ideas that our mind believes to be the truth. Yet they can be a funnel of guidance to unleash our divine potentials and abilities. As your fears arise, observe them and do not judge yourself. Make peace with them by acknowledging and allowing them to condense like the morning dew's determination to reach the sky. Release the fears that are blocking your potential to experience the endless possibilities available in the world. Apply yourself with confidence and courage. You are an unlimited soul.

Actualize your power. There is a flow of immense potential sleeping deeply in your mind. It is waiting to be unraveled, but first you must quit engaging in doubtful conversations with yourself. When you realize your innate abilities, you must become brave to step fully fledged onto your path. In inspiration and motivation, act with little consideration of obstacles and possible limitations coming along the way. The path will be uncomfortable and unclear, but trust the greater force emanating from within. There is nothing holding you back other than what you are saying to yourself. Are you willing to allow your ideas to soar beyond your doubts?

As you realize your power, fear will continually be a factor. It will try to bring up unresolved misconceptions of what you can do, and it may cause missed opportunities or delays along the way. Remember, your ego uses fear as a weapon to keep you secure or to self-sabotage your plans. However, you can use your fears as a blessing to see the underlying power at work on your path. If it does not scare you, then you are not challenging yourself enough to become your greatest unlimited self.

Stay confident in your truth. Stay true to your path and passion. Remain humble and thankful. It is important to always allow your intuition to be the guide when creating and designing a new story. It knows your truth and never strays away into the world of rules and regulations. Your intuitive self keeps a check and balance on your self-confidence to avoid over-zealousness. Remain loyal to the truth of who you are.

Staying in your truth is an important factor to manifest what you desire, because what is meant for you will not disappear or run away. What is meant for you requires patience and diligence. What is meant for you will arrive when you are ready to receive it. Nothing and no one else holds the key to unlocking the power within you but yourself.

If ever you find yourself in an indecisive battle about whether you can achieve a goal, remind yourself that you are self-sufficient, creative, and powerful with God in your plans. Like a chameleon, you can adapt to any environment. For brilliance and resilience emanate from the most wondrous and extraordinary aspects within your subconscious mind. Move in faith and be ready for the amazing breakthroughs with your unlimited essence of self.

> **Leaves of Healing:** *Unlimited Tools to Use*

There is a plethora of divine tools available for use. They are granted by God and serve as indispensable methods to tap into our unlimited nature.

- Incorporate daily meditations and prayers to ask for what you want.
- Write and say your affirmations with confidence to feel your powerful essence.
- Expand and get creative with your visualizations to envision the new, unfolding story on the horizon.
- Chant the beautiful mantras of the Eastern traditions to boost the expansive synergy in connection to every being.

To start the mood, create a simple affirmation, called a fiat, for yourself. Own the fiat; it's free to use anytime. Redesign the fiat to fit your way of remembering the words. Scream it out when you need to apply it in an interview or an aspiring endeavor. Feel your fears dissolving into the air as your unlimited power unleashes from the depths of your soul. Here are a few examples:

I already got this!
I am ready!
It is already done!
I am unlimited!
All is well with God!

IS FOR VALIANT

Branch Val•iant (A): Calling on your inner strength to overcome adversities. Remaining courageous in order to strive during difficult circumstances.

> **Rooted Experience:** *Are you standing firm in your strength during tests and trials of life?*

A year had passed since I moved to New York City from Jamaica. After my first winter experience in New York City, I begged my father to book the next available flight to Kingston at the end of my sophomore year in high school. My body missed the feel of the radiant tropical sun of my former homeland.

As I walked on the streets of my childhood neighborhood in the Waltham Park area of Kingston, nothing had changed since I left. The same curious and at times unfriendly faces of neighbors gazed at me with wondrous looks. The same colorful graffiti was calligraphed on the walls with lists of street crews. The same meager, homeless dogs scuffled for chicken skin and fruit peels discarded by the neighbors. The smell of marijuana and burning trash fumed up my nostrils.

It felt great to return to yaad, as we Jamaicans described our beautiful island.

Schools were out of session and all my former high school friends had already left for their own summer vacations. As much as I tried to enjoy my time, my sixteen-year-old-self became bored with my neighborhood. There were few activities happening in the community that interested me. Therefore, to pass the time I created my own little excursions around town for the remainder of my stay.

My first adventure was to visit my former teachers at St. Hugh's, my previous high school, which was located a short distance away by bus.

"Yuh nuh fraid fi travel alone? Yuh a farrina." Nicole, my childhood friend, asked when I told her of my plans to take the bus.

"Why should I be afraid?" I was a bit confused by her question.

Kingston was my home. I had lived there for fifteen years of my life without concerns about traveling anywhere. As far as I knew, nothing could prevent me from doing what I wanted.

Boarding one of the small, local mini-buses, I gave a huge sigh of relief after securing an available seat at the back. There were fewer passengers there compared to the crowd of people clustered at the front. Dropping myself in the nearest window seat, I looked outside and smiled as the hot breeze blew through the rusted air-vents.

I can't wait to see them, I thought of my former teachers. But my daydream was interrupted by a young passenger.

"Excuse me?" I replied to the small skinny boy who looked around my age. He sat a few shoulders away from me and wore ripped jeans with a black and white bandana tied around his head.

His close proximity unnerved me.

"Gimme your bag or mi will burst your face open," the boy mumbled under his breath as he drew closer to my side.

And without a question or hesitation, I handed him my purse.

Don't panic, Terry. Remain calm, an inner voice whispered. He pocketed all my belongings—fake jewelry, paper to wipe my face from the heat, and the thousand Jamaican adventure money my grandmother gave to me. As he rummaged through my purse, he then attempted to take my permanent resident card—my only pass back to the United States of America. *Wait a moment! He must be crazy! Is he going to walk through the airport pretending to be me?*

"Please leave the card and take everything else." I bluntly asked him. A rage erupted in me from out of nowhere. To my surprise, he listened.

As I spoke out, my eyes caught the presence of another young assailant who sat at the front of the bus while his friend robbed me. His frail skinny hands positioned the muzzle of a hidden gun under his faded T-shirt toward me.

I breathed heavily in fear but felt an inner knowing that the gun was only a scare tactic to keep me quiet. But the gun did not bother me as much as the large kitchen knife lodged on the seat next to my waist. The young boy was still ravaging through my scanty purse and seemed to have no intention to leave anything.

Oh God! Get me out of here! My hands trembled. They eye-signaled each other, paid their fare to the conductor, and got off at the next stop. Tears flowed in disappointment as I watched them running down the street with my adventure funds.

Frightened. Shocked. Angry. I alerted the conductor of the robbery. But, with an unbelievable lack of judgement, the conductor showed no sympathy to my dilemma and demanded that I pay my fare regardless of what had happened. A rage broiled within me but I sighed deeply for inner strength and patience to avoid any confrontation. Dipping my hands into my breasts—my grandmother's secret method—I gave him the last fifty Jamaican dollars I had.

With no money or idea what to do next, I would not allow this interference to darken my plans. I sucked it up and continued my adventure to see my former teachers as planned. Even though the young bandits stole my money and the bus driver took my last dime, I still managed to complete my excursions of the day.

No matter what was taken from me, life went on. The experience only strengthened my inner courage to move past difficult situations.

Rainstorms flood the roots of the Ceiba tree. Thunder rumbles in the distant sky and scares the young harpy hatchling nested in the crown. Lightning strikes and sends weak branches falling to the ground. Despite the elemental dangers, the sacred Ceiba tree stands tall in its strength and power.

The Ceiba tree has weathered the worst of the storms in the tropical rainforests. Yet it remains firm in its stance as it extends its umbrella-crown branches toward the radiant sun. Although the soil is unstable beneath its buttressed roots, the tree secures itself to the ground with confidence. And while the healing leaves disappear during the dry season, it continues to bloom bountiful flowers and bear new fiber-filled fruits.

In every trying situation, find your inner Ceiba of resilience and valiance. Whatever experience blows your way, you can persevere through the storms and conquer your obstacles. In all the tests sent on your path, you have the inner power to move ahead. The fights for survival. The unexpected struggles of life. The hardships endured. They may dim your spirit for a while, but never give them the power to block your inner progress and growth.

Be in valiance at the height of every precarious and challenging time. Your bravery stems from overcoming the difficulties experienced along the way. Never allow temporary adversities to trap you into misery and discontentment about life. With divine guidance and protection, utilize your courage to move past those negative rooted experiences. You can transform your struggles into adventures if you open yourself to the inner warrior.

There is a spirited warrior within yourself; do you feel it? It is ready to unleash when plots of the enemy aim to trample you to the ground. But aim to see those experiences as insights gained. If a challenge did not happen, then how would you know your true strength?

This strength is majestic and towers any negative experience. Like a lotus flower blossoms from muddy waters, you can blossom in love, confidence, and trust. God knows you have been cheated, robbed, bruised, beaten, and neglected in the world, but the Divine gave you inner strength to withstand those tests with courage. Negative situations can only have power over you if you allow them to.

Day in, day out, there will be tests. Tests of patience. Tests of love. Tests of forgiveness. Life is not about what others have done to you but how you react to the moment and bounce back. Allow your emotions to flow, but never allow them to steer you off your path. The storm clouds may surround you, but your powerful light can pierce through them. You came a long way from where you were. You stood up for your freedom, and now here you are. You are not alone and are divinely protected every day. Call upon the power of God to keep you safe and take control of the issues causing you dismay.

Remember, as we are temporary and subject to change, so is every obstacle. Be strong in your faith, because you can rise beyond any situation. You are a courageous soul who has surpassed the battles, so never give in to negative issues in your life. Once you remain in faith, you can only discover that your inner courage strikes magnificence even in those stormy moments.

Leaves of Healing: *Thundering Strength Affirmations*

Do you know how courageous you are? Every obstacle and trial that you have conquered brought you to this very point in time. The best is yet to come, but the worse will still show up. Face it. Push through it. Use your thundering inner strength to break the chains of fear and blockages. Wherever you feel comfortable, whether it is in your living room, in your bedroom, or even in your car, I want you to thunder strike every obstacle using your right index finger as a wand. Shout the below affirmations aloud:

I have pushed past my obstacles!

I have conquered my fears!

I have surpassed the tests and adversities!

I have unlocked the power of valiance with God in my life!

IS FOR WORTH

Branch Worth (A): Staying with your self-love. Your self-respect. Your self-confidence. Putting more value in yourself because you deserve better.

Rooted Experience: *Do you recognize your own self-worth?*

Saturday mornings in Jamaica entailed cleaning every room in our small two-bedroom house in Kingston.

I lived with my grandmother and two brothers in a tenement unit, which was occupied by different residents from all walks of life, all of whom rented their own separate housing section on the enormous shared plot of land.

In these living arrangements, I eavesdropped on almost every piece of gossip, witnessed many domestic disagreements over clothesline spaces, and enjoyed the shouts and laughter of domino nights. Yet none compare to one of my most memorable experiences, which involved eavesdropping on the ongoing drama between Miss Mary and her daughter, Cassandra, at the public washstand underneath my grandmother's bedroom window.

"Hey! Likkle gyal, yuh have no common sense," Miss Mary shouted at her daughter. I peeped through the window and saw little Cassandra walking towards her mother with a bucket filled with water.

"Move with some life in yuh body!" She slapped Cassandra across the face. I could not imagine how a skinny eight-year-old girl was able to carry such a large bucket in those tiny hands while being a punching bag. She must have been stronger than I was, as no tears dripped from her stunned eyes.

"Move faster! Put the pan over there!" Miss Mary shouted again. With every scream, I cringed at the sound of her squeaking voice, which stung my eardrums.

As I peeped at them, I noticed the usual aggravated lines on Miss Mary's face. *Why is she always angry? Why does she shout all the time? Why does she curse Cassandra for no reason at all?* I wondered. Each time I saw Ms. Mary, whether at the washstand or on the street, there was a sad look in her eyes and an angriness in her voice. Perhaps they were due to the quarrels she had had last night with her on-and-off-again boyfriend, Sam. Whatever the reasons were for her aggressive attitude, it was too bad Cassandra usually had to suffer for her mother's frustration.

With her hands dripping with suds from the laundry detergent, Ms. Mary dipped the clothes in the bucket with anger. In and out. In and out. As she did this, she cursed on and on about life's unfairness. She ranted about not having enough money, about Sam's cheapness and lies, and about the same story of Cassandra being of no help to her.

"You have no use, whatsoever. Very wukless," she told Cassandra, while trying to make space for another resident who had joined the wash area with loads of laundry.

Wukless is a Jamaican way of saying someone is worthless. Useless. Incapable. I heard this term a lot as a child, and it felt degrading and belittling to hear someone calling me those words. I knew it affected Cassandra as well. As she stood with her head lowered to the ground waiting for the next directives from her mother, she positioned her tiny body to be ready for the worst degradation yet to come.

Striking up a conversation with the other unknown female

resident, Ms. Mary started to describe her daughter's current "use" in her life.

Who's that? I had never seen this new woman before. Yet I was not surprised, since faces changed often in the tenement yard.

"Bwoy, I'm telling you," she shook her head.

"This likkle gyal is growing up with no common sense. She caan [cannot] do nothing. She caan wash. She caan clean. She has no use in life." Ms. Mary informed the glossy-eyed female resident.

Adding her two cents, the woman concurred. "Yes, yes. Mine is the same. This generation of vipers have nothing about them. They have no use whatsoever."

My stomach turned listening to them, as they cackled on about how children were useless and worthless, as if we were not human. It saddened my heart to see Cassandra standing there, unable to defend herself as they fed a myriad of negative comments into her head. By the look on her face and in her eyes, I could tell that she was embarrassed and ashamed.

Yet the more I listened to them, the more I noticed how much they seemed to dislike their own lives. The cheating men. The lack of money. The jealousy and gossip about other female residents. They discussed everything happening in their lives except their own unhappiness with themselves. The more they fussed and complained, the more their words fell heavy on my mind.

They did not realize that they projected negativity towards Cassandra and unknowingly to me.

Leaving the window to finish my chores, I shook my head in sadness for the hopes of children who suffered belittlement from their own parents or any adults. I promised myself to never allow anyone—not even family—to bring me down to their own level of self-conviction. For I knew I was worth more than what they projected in fear. My one wish was that Cassandra recognized that as well.

Only you can create your own definitions on the branches of your inner Ceiba. Never allow others to determine your self-worth and value. You are worth more than what you have been told by anyone or experienced in your lifetime. Understand your importance and what you are meant to be in the present moment. You control your own happiness; do what makes you content and embrace your inner freedom. Shine your own light and step forward in confidence. Rise beyond what others may believe or have said about you. Your self-worth is your freedom to be yourself.

Most times what we carry as negative self-worth derives from the thoughts and words projected by another person, especially from our loved ones. It can be depressing to listen to a family member, a friend, or a partner feed us negativity about what they may think about their own reality. Never feel like a victim or ashamed of who you are because of someone else's fear and own self-judgment. At times, they are just trying to transfer their sadness, despair, or bitterness toward you. Keep in mind that others can only define you as much as you allow them to do so. Take back your power by realizing your self-worth and staying true to yourself.

You have control of what you accept as truth and how you define the words others say to you. Like branches can be broken down to twigs, words can be broken down back to its origin to recreate a newly defined experience.

Instead of feeling useless or worthless, use less of your time and value feeding anyone's negative projections. This means if someone calls you "worthless" or "useless," aim to *use less* of your attention to pleasing them and more to building your own happiness. Create a new perception about a word to shine a different light in living a better reality. It is your inner Ceiba, and only you can define your words.

Understand that you are priceless, highly favored, and worthy to receive the best. Give yourself the love and appreciation to move forward with confidence. When you use your inner courage to surpass negative encounters with anyone, you can only blossom in your true self. As you move on with your life, what you say or think of yourself becomes of greater significance in understanding and embracing your self-worth. So make the effort each day to give yourself the recognition and love you truly deserve.

Leaves of Healing: *Know Your Worth Affirmations*

You are precious. You are divine. You are more valuable than dime. How you view yourself is reflected in your experiences. Change your words to evoke a new wave of self-confidence in yourself. Instead of saying or thinking "I am useless," transform those decaying thoughts to healing leaves by affirming, "I am worthy and use less of my time supporting people who choose to bring me down." In addition to that, recite the below affirmations to remind yourself of how important and loved you are.

I use less of my time on who or what does not serve my purpose.

I use more of my value in building my self-confidence.

I am worthy and deserving of true peace and happiness.

I love and embrace my divine self.

IS FOR XTRAORDINARY

Branch X tr·aordi·nar·y (A): Uncanny. Special. Unique and different beyond the norms of society.

> **Rooted Experience:** *Are you willing to embrace your "weird" traits?*

I f someone paid me one hundred dollars for each time I've been described as a weirdo or being "out there," or an oddball, I would be a millionaire by now. I remember the labels like they were yesterday—as a matter of fact, some of them were very recent.

I recalled the "Terry is a wairdo" message scribbled on the wall of the girls' bathroom in high school. *The audacity*, I thought, appalled at the erroneous spelling of *weirdo* written next to my name.

I recalled the "Terry is so eccentric and creepy" whispers from colleagues who would engage in common break-room gossip. *I guess I'm doing well.* I smiled in amazement. My reserved and introverted nature seemed to have made a great impression on my work partners. It felt good to know that I was the center of other individuals' priorities.

Over the years I wondered why my colleagues or family members, or even people who barely knew me, questioned the way I looked or expressed myself. I wondered why they felt drawn to highlight my supposed weirdness. At one point I thought, *Perhaps I need to fit in with the crowd and act normal for a change.* But each time I tried to adjust myself to other people's opinions, my soul plunged me into negative experiences as a reminder to remain true to who I was.

Ok, Terry, admit it. You are far from the ordinary, I acknowledged. The more others emphasized how eccentric I was, through gossip or comedic pursuits, the more I realized it was not meant to change anything about me. They were only pointing out the qualities I did not acknowledge about my own self. Their comments were meant to be a push, motivation, and reignition of the "weird" parts of myself, the parts I failed to see or had pushed away out of fear of judgment.

Nonetheless, as the whispers and negative comments rolled through my ears, I utilized them as a source of empowerment to explore more about who I am. When I am called strange or odd, I clench to every word as a sign or symbol that I am doing well on my path. The more I adapt to the negativity, the more I embrace my extraordinary abilities.

Trunk Insight: *Embrace Your Xtraordinary Self Without Fear*

Have you taken some level of algebra in school? Do you recall when your math teacher would ask to "find x" in class? From what I remembered in my earlier college years, most students disliked the steps to finding x, for some unknown reason. Was it due to the fear of math or what they would rather not try to understand? Or did the path to deciphering that x seem confusing and uncomfortable to begin with? Whatever the reasons were, they still had to find x to arrive at the answer.

In an academic setting, finding x involves many known variables and formulas with set rules and orders of operation. However, in the school of life, finding your x entails no rules or formulas but being bold enough to traverse your insecurities attached to what it means to be normal.

Your x is your extraordinary natural self, connecting you to your truth. It is a branch we, at times, choose not to walk in life out of fear of ridicule and judgment from others. The complex factors of embracing our extraordinary self tends to include how we perceive ourselves in the eyes of our peers. Sometimes these outlooks are quite negative and leave us adjusting our persona to fit into certain environments.

However, why should you adjust who you are to acclimate to an environment? Why should you compromise yourself to be normal just to fit into a group? If someone highlights your abnormalities, use their words as an advantage to tap into your powers. Despite the limited construct existent in the "You are creepy and weird" outlook, use these factors to break away from the old belief systems surrounding what is normal or acceptable.

The fears of "What if they laugh at me?" or "What if I'm shut out of my community?" can be scary and uncomfortable. However, they may help you to identify a unique part of yourself you had feared to express from your soul. If this happens, see past the labels and allow them to serve as variables to assist you in unraveling the natural extraordinary power within yourself.

God gave everyone abilities and skills to create better experiences for themselves. This feat can be accomplished when one travels their own unique path with less consideration of critics and judgments. Do not hide what God has given to you to shine forth into the world.

We are intelligent creators. In today's modern world, we have superseded our own fears to create what our ancestors could not accomplish in their time. From towering skyscrapers to ingenious self-driving cars to the creative expression of music and literature, we are remarkable souls capable of infinite possibilities. These accomplishments highlight the power of human capabilities beyond our societal constrictions. There is a wealth of internal information to disseminate, but you must choose to integrate your own uniqueness, even if you appear weird from another individual's periphery.

Having said that, we are all collectively working together to add to the growth and development of life. We should learn to respect the weirdness within ourselves and others because we may need them to guide us in trying times. There is a divine purpose attached to the utmost part of our weirdness. We should only expand in our extraordinary nature and not allow ourselves to contract into insecurities of what society would think. In God's plan, you were created to be a leader in your own strangeness not a follower in the crowd of normalcy.

Leaves of Healing: *Find your X Questions and Answers*

Do you recall a rooted experience when you have been called weird or odd? How did you feel? If the experience felt liberating, then you are already walking the branch of x. If the experience felt degrading, then you can transform it into a path of positivity and a source of empowerment. Acknowledge how you feel about the remarks; do not deny them. You can turn your weird nature into extraordinary greatness. Here are a few questions to ask yourself as you rediscover your x:

What is my x? *Sample Answer*: My x is my extraordinary nature, connected to the untapped abilities or qualities within myself. I am yet to tune into and embrace this side of me because I am still learning to transcend societal labels and categories.

How can I embrace my x? *Sample Answer*: I accept who I am. I move beyond my comfort zones. I express myself in the direction of love and truth.

How can my x make a difference? *Sample Answer*: With my x, I add value to the world. By embracing more of my truth, I help others who may also fear going beyond norm to express themselves. As I walk this branch, I demonstrate that ridicule can become empowerment and can help one to rediscover one's own extraordinary self.

IS FOR YOUTHFUL

Branch Youth·ful (A): Be playful as much as you can. Engage in more fun and leisure as you work to create your life.

Rooted Experience: *Are you engaging in more play?*

Beep beep beep! The fax machine went off in the copy room a few feet away from my cubicle. The loud notification interrupted my trail of thoughts, which was focused on completing the outstanding financial reports from two weeks ago. I had been scrambling to finish them, since they were due to the budget office by the end of the business day.

Beep beep beep! It went again. "Ugh! Where's everyone? I have work to do here."

Before another annoying sound rang through my eardrums, I stormed out of my chair towards the copy room to turn off the ruckus the machine was creating. *What could be so important?* I rolled my eyes at the incoming message sent with such urgency.

"Need a vacation right away?? Book a $99 round-trip flight to Jamaica, Cancun, or the Cayman Islands." *Really, is this what I left my desk for?* I ripped the paper apart and returned to work. It was 2:00 p.m. on a dreary and gloomy Monday afternoon, and my attention span had already wandered off into a blank space.

Not only did the disruption break my focus, but I was overwhelmed and nowhere close to finalizing the reports.

Damn! I guess I will stay late, I pouted, as my tired eyes faded to the keyboard. My hands grew weary from typing too fast and my neck stiffened like a log. Lounging back in my chair with my fingers crossed on the back of my head, I yelled out, "I need a vacation!" But the possibilities of traveling anywhere anytime soon seemed far-fetched with all the projects I had on my plate.

The last time I had taken a well-needed vacation was during a brief rendezvous to Miami Beach, Florida with an ex-lover in the summer of 2016. Even though the trip was adventurous, it was too short to experience much fun. The three days I expended were not enough compared to if I had taken at least a week off from work. I did not want to leave my responsibilities unchecked for too long.

Working full-time as a manager, finishing up my master's degree in economics, and supporting my grandmother in Jamaica were not easy responsibilities to manage. They became more of a priority than planning vacation trips or having fun in general. My mind constantly went back and forth in, *Who would handle my work? Who would complete the assigned reports if I am not there? Who would answer the questions if my boss asked?* With all that was happening around me, time off seemed next to "Neveruary" in my plans.

When the weekend arrived, rest and relaxation were all my mind and body craved. After scrambling through the work week filled with deadlines and meetings, I was depleted from the mental exhaustion and tingling muscle pains. *Damn!* I panicked. A sudden ton of stress nerved through me. I could not recall whether I had submitted the right versions of the reports to my boss.

"I cannot live like this!" I blurted out as I sat in the sofa with a cup of mango ice cream. It irked me to know that my weekly life involved more work, more school, little sleep, and more exhaustion.

Beep! An unexpected text from my phone reminded of the annoying fax machine from earlier. Cheryl, a long-time friend of the family, reached out with a smiling emoji girl. As I read through the texts, she extended a warm invitation to travel with her and some friends to Cuba.

Whoa, Cuba! I always wanted to go there! Instantly, my mood shifted away from my life's problems and piling priorities. With the current travel ban lifted from President Obama's administration, the invitation seemed to be a once-in-a-lifetime opportunity. *Snap out of it!* my ego mind interjected, reminding me of all the bills left to pay and the pending projects at work. However, my soul wanted to escape it all. My mind and body needed a break from the automated lifestyle. *Just do it*, an inner voice prompted. And without further ado, I accepted her invite and prepared for a long overdue vacation to Havana, Cuba.

Hola Havana. Here I come!

Leaving the February wintry mix of NYC, I boarded the first available JetBlue flight on its way to Havana. My melanin-toned body greeted the radiance of the warm Cuban sunshine as I stepped out of the airport. My smile welcomed the encapsulating stare from Cuban people's faces. The moment never felt so real and so alive.

As the trip progressed forward, five other ladies and I indulged in all the varying activities available throughout the country. From an epic ziplining stunt in Viñales Valley to exploring ancient Indian caverns to riding in a 1950s pink Chevrolet classic convertible with a handsome Cuban chaperone, we embraced every single adventure as much as we could.

As for me, thoughts of checking my work emails drifted in but flowed past my mind. Engulfed in the vintage beauty of Havana, the laid-back and reserved nature of the Cuban people reminded me of how I needed to relax and slow it down. I felt guilty that I had forgotten what it meant to take a break, have fun, and enjoy the fruits of my own labor.

Six months after my unforgettable and enlightening trip to Cuba, I accepted another invitation from another friend to visit an entirely different landscape. This time around I sat on a seven-hour flight on my way to the "land of fire and ice," Iceland. Since I did not swim in Cuba, I thought, "Hmm. Why not swim in the sizzling warmth of a geothermal pool?"

And so there I was. My body was submerged in the natural hot spring from Mother Nature while my eyelashes and hair formed icicles in the ten-degrees-Fahrenheit temperature. Feeling frozen but contented, I pranced around with my new friends in the glorious heat springing from the volcanic rocks beneath my feet. As I splashed and played around, I thanked God for the moment to be youthful.

Trunk Insight: *You Only Live Once: Live It Now!*

The broad, aging leaves of the Ceiba open themselves to bask in the magical radiance of the sunlight. When the wind hits the branches, the leaves sway back and forth in a dancing, whimsical spirit. In an effortless flow, there is an encapsulating playfulness and wonder in the leaves' movement. Like the Ceiba's leaves, set the intent to dance, flow, and play in your divine youthfulness.

Your youthful nature does not constitute your physical age, abilities, or beauty. It is a wondrous, loving, and childlike energy emerging from your heart and soul. To experience this powerful branch, you must incorporate more play and fun activities into your life. And if you choose to engage in its vibrant buoyancy, you can only achieve more balance and peace in your mind, body, and spirit.

To become youthful is to embrace the inner child. Your inner child is the version of you that has been pushed to the background because of work priorities or school obligations or simply because you created no time for it. As you engage with this precious side of yourself, you can only enhance the quality of your life from a fresh and uplifting perspective. You may broaden your horizon to newer and greater heights in living your life to its fullest.

When you trek the branch of Youthfulness, living in the moment, laughing just for fun, and loving like there is no tomorrow becomes your way of life. This may alter your imagination to a state of bliss and gratitude. Allow yourself to be more playful as you breathe the air and allow the sun to illuminate your beautiful being. To experience the true nature of life, play as often as you can, even if you create it all in your mind.

Feel yourself standing at the shoreline where the ocean water rushes to the beach. Feel your toes sink into the clear pristine water as it dances along your feet. Feel the wind and rain flowing on your skin as you walk into nature's wonder. Grasp it. Claim it. Own it. Seize every amazing opportunity of fun-filled moments that God bestowed on you to enjoy your life and not suffer in workloads.

Your mind may say "I cannot afford that luxury" or "I don't have the time." However, you created the time for work because of the bountiful benefits. Create an incentive for why you need more play as you live your life. Remember, playfulness is a divine gift. It should not feel like a task to pursue an uncharted territory. Your own health, happiness, and joy depend on that creative and adventurous experience. With all the hard work and dedication you put toward your dreams and wishes, do you not believe that you deserve a bit more play in your life?

There is an adventure broiling in your heart that you may have longed for. No matter how wild or temporary or weird that experience may be, enjoy it while you can, because life changes without notice. Nothing is ever guaranteed. We have no idea what the future holds tomorrow. Having said that, live today in freedom, love, and playfulness. Grasp every given moment for yourself as you enjoy and live your life in youthfulness.

Leaves of Healing: *Get-Away Visualizations*

Close your eyes. Take a moment to breathe in peace and breathe out stress. Now, imagine yourself on a beautiful, white sand beach in Bali, Jamaica, or Hawaii, or visualize yourself overlooking the valley in a mountainous area in Norway, India, or South Africa. You can also visualize yourself doing whatever activity sparks your interest, stirs your heart, and ignites fun and excitement into your life. It does not matter where your adventurous soul takes you, just ensure that you are playing and enjoying your life for a change. As you hone into the visualizations, picture yourself already there. Can you feel it? Say to yourself, "Yes! I feel it! I want it! I'm already living it!" Now, open your eyes and go make it happen in your reality. What are you waiting for? The excitement of life awaits you.

IS FOR ZEALOUS

Branch Zeal•ous (A): Enthusiastic toward building your life with passion and effort. Moving forward with due diligence while exercising mindfulness with others.

> **Rooted Experience:** *Are you mindful of others*
> *as you work toward an outcome?*

Unchecked flags of financial deadlines popped up on my email task bar. This created much unneeded anxiety for the work week ahead. I had been dreading the unmet budget goals, which were still pending projects in my notebook. *It's official!* I thought to myself. *This is one of the most stressful business weeks ever.*

With all that was going on, I still managed to get work done. If it had not been for the dedication and commitment of my professional team, meeting the weekly budget deadlines would have been an utmost impossibility. As a finance manager, it was difficult to tackle every project assignment alone in a short period of time. In confidence and trust, I relied on other professionals to work their skillful magic. Although their appointment papers called me supervisor, in our work space we were all colleagues and equals.

Taking the role of a leader was not an easy feat. It required mutual respect, humbleness, and an unwavering patience with employees, even in times when misunderstandings and mindless reactions arise.

As I ruffled through the pile of paperwork on my desk from previous weeks, I noticed that something was different in my pending trays. I stumbled across a colorful flyer with my name printed on it.

Bolded in red, it noted "Terry Wisdom is an asshole manager."

Wait a minute! What the hell? I was stung by the contents of the details written about me. The flyer was posted by a former team member who had resigned a few weeks earlier, after multiple miscommunications between him and me. Frozen in my chair, I continued to read the dreadful notes and messages he wrote.

"Terry is rude and unprofessional. She abuses her power." The unfathomable descriptions painted a monstrous picture of me as a leader, which was far from the person I knew within myself.

This is not happening. I panicked while I tried to keep calm. The terrible nature of his words caused an immediate fear that was damaging the core of my professional reputation and piercing my heart like thorns.

Pondering on my next movement, I could not imagine what my other colleagues thought. I peeped over my cubicle and noticed that the staff had received the flyers as well. With their jaws wide open, they were now focusing their attention towards me. Like milk boiling over on a hot stove, a surge of embarrassment, anger, and shame trickled over me.

There was nothing left to do but to walk out of the office with my head lowered in distress. Rushing to the restroom, I attempted to hold myself together. But as soon as I entered the first stall, the tears ran wildly like the Orinoco rapids.

Wow I cannot believe he would go this far! I bawled and shook my head in horror. My day and unfinished week had warped into a wicked and cruel dark comedy. *You've done nothing wrong,* an inner voice whispered to soothe my inner and outer turmoil. However, the storm of the moment was too unbearable and carried my thoughts away in despair and victimhood. The only viable option at that point was to return to my desk with a heavy heart dragging to the floor, wishing I could flush away what I had just seen.

The day went by slowly in the office. I tried to tune out the whispers around me. Once I got home, I plunged to the ground as a flood of tears raged out of me. *I cannot do this anymore! I'm done with people!* I shouted to God.

Drowning in my own sorrows, I began to plan my exit.

Are you giving up? Pull your damn self together! An inner voice screamed at me. Deep within I knew crying over the erupting issue would not alleviate the situation or make it vanish. Facing the storm head on, in strength and faith, was the best available option.

The next day I arose with a sense of peace and calmness. As I entered the office, I prepared for the next dramatic episodes to unfold into chaos.

To my surprise, the day took an unexpected turn.

Met with bright smiles and unwavering support, I received a plethora of feedback from many of my colleagues.

"He's only jealous of your success as a black woman," a top executive noted to me as she shared a similar story in her twenty-year-plus experience as a manager.

"You're young and new to this, so people will play with your emotions and take advantage of you," another managerial colleague denoted. She suggested a course in "dealing with difficult people," to help me overcome the developing situation.

While their advice brought much comfort, it did not change how I felt about what happened between him and me. It did not matter to me whether I was a young manager or a successful black woman.

What mattered the most was understanding the role I had played in attracting such a daunting experience.

Was I mindless in my interaction with him? I thought about the times we had worked on one-on-one projects. *Did I fail to see things from a different perspective?* My mind replayed moments when he had argued with me because of misunderstandings. It was apparent that we did not see eye to eye on many things.

Nonetheless, I had accepted that I had no control in how he felt towards me but I had ultimate control in how I reacted at any point during our engagements. What occurred that day shifted my mindset in dealing with others on a more conscious level. As I worked toward my goals, I kept an open mind and incorporated more emotional wisdom, even with the most difficult people.

The storm of that experience left internal and external remnants on its path, but it never damaged or lessened the true essence of who I was. I embraced that moment as a lesson in emotional wisdom to help me emerge as an effective leader. And as time healed and passed, I grew wiser when dealing with others—not because of my last name, but from embracing a different kind of zeal with wisdom and compassion.

Trunk Insight: *As You Co-create With Others, Incorporate Emotional Wisdom*

We are zealous by nature; there is no doubt about this. We all possess this motivating and, at times, misconstrued trait within ourselves. Often, when we hear the word itself, our minds tend to associate it with an overconfident, narcissistic, or arrogant individual. Yet, being zealous is more about designing our lives while working in unison with others.

When we are passionate about a dream or aspiration, our zealous nature becomes a dynamic flow of creative energy which we can be utilized to push us forward. At the same time, if there is no mindfulness in our engagement with other persons, this branch will fall apart. Therefore, it is important that we balance our interactions with the people around us. Emotional wisdom is a necessary element as we dedicate and commit ourselves to the path forward.

Emotional wisdom is the ability to use conscious discernment. Following our dreams with passion should work in hand in hand with respect. Yes, we want to push through on a task, but we must be considerate of the people involved. If we allow ourselves to become mindless in our engagements, then our ego will take charge and create chaotic situations. Zeal partnered with our ego can cause unwanted dramas. Zeal connected to our soul fuels more balance, success, and flow.

Inner zeal fueled by our soul's power creates emotional wisdom and understanding of the bigger picture of our goals. In mindfulness, you can achieve better results and blossom trustworthy future partnerships in your experiences. Always remember that wisdom and understanding are powerful guides in the co-creative endeavors, even during episodes of unfriendly engagements. We can learn to work with the people around us, even if they have been belligerent, deceptive, or manipulative. At the end of the day, you hold the key to your own emotions and actions, so charge your zeal with mindfulness.

When one is not mindful, the diligent force of a zealous nature can become attached to the ego. When this happens, our mind spills over in arrogance, which can become destructive to ourselves and others. To balance our interaction as we create our desired reality, we must integrate our inner guidance and align ourselves the purest intentions and actions. There is little to no wisdom when the ego is in control of creating an experience. Let your intuition be the driver and allow your ego to ride along in the back seat. Remember, your passions and goals are no better than the people who assist you in making it a reality.

As you work towards achieving what you want, learn to work with others by not taking matters personally. Situations may not always work this way, but continue to embrace mindfulness all the same. Be conscious in your interactions, even with the people who sought to bring you to your knees. The more you align with the zeal from your soul, not from your ego, the better you will attract the people who will be more aligned to your heart's passion and soul's purpose. Remain dedicated to your path always, with continued enthusiasm and a twist of emotional wisdom.

Leaves of Healing: *A Zeal Decree*

As you pursue your plans, always be considerate of others in the creative process. No one person can accomplish a feat without the collective strength of its community. All great pioneers and leaders recognize this wisdom as they manifest their own dreams. Now say the below decree to yourself and set clear intentions and healthy boundaries with others, but with appreciation and kindness. Keep these words close to you, whether at work or at home. Let them act as a reminder that you work in connection with everyone as God intended.

I create the life I want with love and compassion.

I move forward with my goals with consideration for others.

I attain success by connecting with my intuition, not my ego self.

& NOW YOU KNOW

Did you think Z was the end? Of course not. How many times did you sung the ABC phonics song before you finally memorized the flow of the letters and used it to its full effect? Even now, you still utilize your ABCs to simplify your phone contacts, your checklists, and your file cabinets. Repetition is key here. You must repeat and repeat the process before you can fully grasp the power and flow of your inner Ceiba.

The Maya recognized that our world, the Universe, and even our own thoughts and physical bodies operate under a cycle. Your inner Ceiba is exactly that, a spiraling dynamic cycle of inner transformations, lessons, and new beginnings. The more you utilize the words and tools, the more you create a different perspective on your experiences. To incorporate your ABCs, you must continually tap into the power of the Ceiba tree by **SAYING**, **BECOMING**, and **APPLYING** the branch definitions with heightened awareness.

A. SAY the words.

Use the power of affirmations, prayers, mantras, or chants to allow the divine energy within your soul to flow into your life. The mere utterance of these words with intent and belief can bring profound changes to one's perspective over time. As you affirm the words and their definitions, integrate them as part of your daily speech. They can become more ingrained in your vocabulary and way of living, if you make the effort. What you say often to yourself is actual energy manifesting into your existence.

B. BECOME the definitions.

You are more than what your rooted experiences have shown you. As you attune to the wisdom of your higher self, return to the truth and light of unconditional love for others and yourself. Become the light of love, joy, and happiness to help redefine and recreate better experiences. Allow the beauty of God's graceful light to seep into your heart and permeate your entire being. The more you flow from the rooted experiences to the branches of better definitions, the more you elevate your awareness to achieve balance in your inner dialogue. To become your inner Ceiba is to flow with life's lesson beyond your old thoughts and word patterns.

C. APPLY the healing leaves often.

Practice is progression and can create immense shifts in one's mindset to allow profound transformations. We must always aim to practice what we wish for. Apply your words as much as you can by putting the leaves of healing into action for at least twenty-six days. No master became a master through one episode of learning but through discipline, commitment, and repetition. Feel the shift in yourself realigning back to love, balance, and wisdom. There are no limitations with your ABCs. Say, become, and apply them as much as can.

Let your 'ABC' Journey Begin...

It is your choice if you want to revamp any conditioned beliefs about what you can create for yourself. It is your choice if you want to release those negative thought patterns that are keeping you stagnant and restricted in old ways of living your life. It is your choice if you want to transform the old rooted stories into branches of Love, Center, Trust, and Empowerment. Your life can transform for the better when you take back your power and change your perceptions about your experiences.

Walk the branches of ABCs to grasp and apply the newly created definitions. Face those rooted experiences with openness and acceptance to reevaluate the memories shaping your present existence. Climb up the trunk insight to gain the lessons learned for your soul's expansion. Feed your mind with the leaves of healing to reprogram those old thought and word patterns. And, like a butterfly, you can evolve in greater strength and wisdom, only to recognize that you are more than what your life has taught and will continue to teach you. It is your life. It is your words. It is always your choice. Start utilizing the power of your ABCs and take back control of your life.

"Words are like branches. The more you extend them in truth, the more love sprouts from the roots."

Terry K. Shaw

Ode to the ABCs

I accept who I am and change what I can.
I am beautiful from the inside out.
I am centered in mind, body, and soul.
I am different and uniquely connected to everyone.
I am empowered to move beyond the struggles of life.
I forgive myself and others for any past pain and hurt.
I am grateful for everything God has given to me.
I am honest about who I am.
I am intuitive by nature and not controlled by my ego.
I am jovial despite the obstacles I face in life.
I am kind regardless of how anyone treats me.
I love myself first and foremost, before I give love to another.
I magnetize better experiences as I create my own story.
I am naturally flowing with God as my guidance.
I open my mind and heart to flow into the unknown.
I am patient with the process as my fruits bear in my garden.
I quiet the mental traffic jam of thoughts.
I give respect regardless if I receive it or not.
I am successful as I follow my own passion and purpose.
I trust in God's plan despite my own fears.
I am unlimited in my steps to success and happiness.
I am valiant with inner strength and courage.
I am worthy of the best and honor my heart.
I am xtraordinarily weird—who wants to be normal anyway?
I am youthful and live my life in spontaneity.
I remain zealous in pursuit of my dreams with mindfulness in the mix.

ACKNOWLEDGMENTS

With utmost gratitude and a teary eye, I want to thank every person who has contributed to making this book a dream come true beyond my wild imagination. To my editors, Danielle Baldwin at DBB Advisors, Christopher Hoffmann at Copy Write Consultants, and Carolyn Williams-Noren, all your constructive feedback expanded the book concept to another level. To Brianna Gooch, front cover illustrator, and Ryan Scheife at Mayfly Design, both your creative insights and expertise helped bring my 'scribbled tree' drawings and outlines to life. To my soul family and friends, your continued support and love kept me focused on the vision when I wanted to give up. To the persons who have inspired the contents in this guide, you have taught me a great deal about myself. To Oreo, my furry spirit guide, your constant meows at 2:00 a.m. reminded me to stop writing and go to bed. Last and never least, I give thanks to God and my higher self, who guided me with unwavering trust and patience in this frightening yet fulfilling and blissful process.

Terry K. Shaw is an author, inspirational speaker, and spiritual teacher. She is also the co-author of *Lessons From My Grandmother's Lap: An Anthology* compiled by Regina 'Sunshine' Robinson. Since her spiritual awareness heightened in 2017, Terry has made it her life's path and mission to inspire as many people as she can from around the globe using her words of wisdom and spiritual gifts. She offers daily uplifting messages, healing tips, and insights on her Facebook and Instagram pages. She currently lives in Nutley, New Jersey with Oreo, her furry tuxedo kitty. To find out more about Terry's work, visit www.terryshawinspires.com.

CPSIA information can be obtained
at www.ICGtesting.com
Printed in the USA
FSHW010249130619
59006FS